Murray Leinster was a prolific writer whose work spans many genres but whose science fiction dominated the later part of his career and included most of his best known work. Algis Budrys was one of the genre's most honored critics and editors, and was also the author of at least three classic novels.

Managansett Press

Don D'Ammassa is the author of

Nonfiction
The Encyclopedia of Science Fiction
The Encyclopedia of Fantasy & Horror
The Encyclopedia of Adventure Fiction
Masters of Detection Vol I*
Masters of Detection Vol II*
Masters of Detection Vol III*
Masters of Detection Vol IV
Masters of Detection Vol V*
Masters of Fantasy
Masters of Horror Vol I*
Masters of Horror Vol II*
Architects of Tomorrow Vol I*
Architects of Tomorrow Vol II*
Architects of Tomorrow Vol III*
Not Exactly a Memoir*

Don D'Ammassa is the author of:

Horror
Blood Beast
Servant of Chaos*
Caverns of Chaos*
Wings over Manhattan
The Gargoyle
That Way Madness Lies*
Little Evils*
Passing Death*
Date with the Dark*
The Devil Is in the Details*
Living Things*
Shadows Over R'Lyeh*
More Shadows Over R'Lyeh*

Science Fiction
Scarab*
Haven*
Narcissus*
Translation Station
The Sinking Island*
Alien & Otherwise*
Wormdance*
Sandcastles*
Carbon Copies*
Phantom of the Space Opera*
The Retro Collection*

Mysteries
Murder in Silverplate*
Dead of Winter*
Death at the Art Gallery*
Death on the Mountain*
Death on Black Island*
Death in Black and White*
Death in the Neighborhood*

Fantasy
The Kaleidoscope*
Elaborate Lies*
The Maltese Gargoyle*
Perilous Pursuits*
Multiplicity*
The Hippogriff of the Baskervilles*
Ten Little Homunculi*

*published by Managansett Press

2

ARCHITECTS OF TOMORROW VOL IV

Managansett Press First Edition 2019

ARCHITECTS OF TOMORROW
VOL IV

CONTENTS

MURRAY LEINSTER

Murray Leinster was the pseudonym of William Fitzgerald Leinster (1896-1975), a prolific author of dozens of books, mostly science fiction but also including westerns, mysteries, and romance novels and a great deal of adventure fiction at shorter length. His 1500 short stories are similarly spread among many genres, although he is best known for his science fiction. He won Hugo awards for his novelette, "Exploration Team," and another for "First Contact," probably his best known story.

Leinster's first sale was to *The Smart Set* magazine in 1916. His first science fiction story was "The Runaway Skyscraper" in 1919. Because of the breadth and volume of his work, a chronological survey would likely be rather confusing, so I will deal with his non-fantastic fiction – which was generally from early in his career – followed by his science fiction novels, and then the short stories. Much of Leinster's short fiction and a few of his early non-SF novels are almost impossible to find today.

Leinster was not noted for a distinct literary style but rather as a story teller. His protagonists are overwhelmingly male although there are occasional strong female characters who contribute more than just a place holder in the story. There are frequent hints of romance but they are never deeply developed and we generally see little of the emotional life of his characters. This is true even in his romance fiction. He was quite versatile, however, and was able to sell fiction to a wide variety of publications and appeal to very divergent editorial tastes. His prose style did not draw attention to itself, but this was deceptive because he was actually very skillful in his plotting and execution.

Writers cannot be separated completely from the world and time in which they were active. During the late 1940s and 1950s Leinster displayed what was then fairly widespread fear of communist subversives and, particularly right after World War II, distrust of even our allies in Europe. Similarly he accepted contemporary stereotyping of gender roles. He was not misogynistic in the sense that he was not virulently disrespectful of women – he had four daughters after all – but he accepted differences in gender and appropriate behavior that would today be considered condescending or patronizing. Despite that mindset, there are several very competent female characters sprinkled through his work.

A short but very fine biography was written by two of his daughters – *Murray Leinster: The Life and Works* by Billee J. Stallings and Jo-an J. Evans (2011). It contains a very large, though not complete, bibliography of his published work.

MYSTERIES

Leinster's mystery novels are virtually unknown and almost impossible to find. They also vary considerably in quality, as might be expected since they were published early in his career. *The Man Who Feared* (1930) was the only one that had a paperback edition. It features James Jarnegan, who is effectively a private investigator although that is not what he calls himself. His prospective new client is J. Grant Harwood, a prominent businessman who indicates that he has been receiving threatening letters. The letter he produces as evidence announces plans to ruin Harwood's life by striking at his friends and family in unspecified ways. Jarnegan refuses to take him as a client, insisting instead that it is police business and not something he feels able to deal with, but also because of some lingering animosity. Harwood and Jarnegan's father were business partners and Harwood took advantage of their relationship. Jarnegan also suspects that there is nothing substantial in the threats until Harwood tells him that a woman friend of his had been murdered the night before, and that the killer called him about it even before the police knew about the crime.

Jarnegan tentatively reconsiders and he and an associate, Ken Talley, visit the scene where the woman, Margery Stone, and her supposed boyfriend died. The landlady is less than helpful and wants no further publicity. The police assume that it was a suicide pact and that the couple turned on the gas and curled up in bed to await their end although there is no obvious motive or suicide note. .

Jarnegan concludes that it was murder and eventually convinces the police that he is right, but Stone and her lover were not important enough that much effort will be put into finding her killer. Jarnegan then meets Harwood's wife, Phyllis, and his sister-in-law, Gloria Hayes. Another threatening but non-specific note arrives promptly. Jarnegan starts looking at Harwood's enemies, but there are quite a lot of them. He does determine that another associate who was believed to have committed suicide was also murdered.

Harwood's safe is broken into and some securities are stolen which technically did not belong to him. This could lead to charges of embezzlement, though Harwood insists – incorrectly – that he did nothing wrong. Harwood also admits that his wife hates him passionately and she becomes a prime suspect. Not much happens for a considerable time except that Jarnegan and Hayes drift toward romance. Then Phyllis Harwood and her secret boyfriend are found dead, obviously removing her from the list of suspects. All evidence of the affair is covered up to protect Harwood's reputation, such as it is.

Jarnegan is worried that Hayes may also be in danger due to her proximity to Harwood, and to a lesser extent, he fears that she may be the one behind the crimes. Harwood asserts at one point that he suspects that Jarnegan himself is his nemesis and holds him at gunpoint, but eventually he reveals that he faked the notes and killed the various people himself in a quest for revenge. Jarnegan outsmarts him and turns the tables.

The plot is not bad, despite a few minor rough spots and the rather sketchy motivation for the crimes. The weakest part of the novel is the pacing, which becomes quite ponderous in the middle third. This could actually have been a much shorter story and would probably have been more effective that way.

Murder Will Out (1933) is an expansion of the short story, "The Purple Hieroglyph," which had been the basis for a silent movie in 1920, *The Purple Cipher*, remade as *Murder Will Out* in 1930, and remade again as *Torchy Blane in Chinatown* in 1939. The screenplay for *Murder Will Out* was by J. Grubb Alexander, who is not credited in the novel published three years later, so it is not clear whether the book is a novelization or an independent expansion but the former is likely making it one of the first film novelizations.

The protagonist is Leonard Staunton, a wealthy man who employs a Chinese valet, Soo Nam. He is engaged to Jeanne Baldwin, a senator's daughter, and is also a close friend of her brother Jack. Staunton receives a visit from another acquaintance named Fitzhugh, who is very much on edge. Fitzhugh tells Staunton that he has been receiving messages threatening to bring about his death at midnight that very day unless he pays a considerable sum of money. The messages have been arriving mysteriously, almost impossibly, and are often accompanied by a drawing of a purple hieroglyph. The similarities to *The Man Who Feared* are obvious, although this is a noticeably better novel.

Staunton joins Fitzhugh at their club just as a thunderstorm knocks out their lights. Jeanne and Jack Baldwin are following and they have an unpleasant encounter with a car full of Chinese men which appears to be coincidental. The deadline seems to pass, but actually all of the clocks in the club have been set forward. When it really is midnight, Fitzhugh is promptly abducted and presumably killed by his abductors.

Lacking a body, the police are reluctant to take the situation seriously. A vacationing British Secret Service officer named Condon has meanwhile found the body, however, floating in a river. The body carries a letter requesting that he be buried at midnight. Condon suspects the letter is a forgery although his reasoning is unclear. A card also shows up bearing a warning to Condon and Staunton to halt their now joint investigation.

The funeral is held and one of those attending, Dr. Mansfield, tells Staunton that he too has received threats against his life from the Chinese extortion ring. Mansfield smokes what appears to be a poisoned cigarette. He immediately diagnoses the poison – completely implausibly – and rushes to his home where he happens to have the specific antidote. The antidote, of course, has been replaced. This clumsy construction is not at all like Leinster and supports the theory that it was part of the screenplay.

Mansfield's body is then stolen right under Condon's nose. Another threatening letter arrives, this time demanding money from Staunton and identifying Jeanne Baldwin as the latest target. Senator Baldwin's mansion is turned into a virtual fortress with federal and private agents guarding the perimeter. Condon also mysteriously receives a death threat from the same source.

Staunton finds a message of his own ordering him to come alone to the pagoda on the grounds at midnight. The secret service prevents him from doing so and Condon goes in his place. The trap is aborted when a small bomb goes off inside the mansion, distracting the people who are supposed to be waiting for Condon's signal. Condon disappears, but a blood stained dagger is found in the pagoda.

Another mysterious message arrives announcing Condon's death and demanding a large ransom to prevent Jeanne's murder. Staunton agrees to deliver the money by boat and does so, but Jack Baldwin is commander of a submarine and he follows. The villains are caught by surprise and unmasked – and they are Fitzhugh, Condon, and

Masters, all very much alive and none of them Chinese. The body in the river was just a ruse. This explains most, but not all, of the miraculously delivered warning messages since the only witnesses to their arrival are in fact members of the gang.

The novel is suspenseful but flawed and the flaws almost certainly resulted from the screenplay. All of the characters refer to the threats as blackmail but they are actually extortion. Some of the unexplained messages are so unlikely that they feel like magic and they are never explained. Condon dismisses them offhandedly: "They manage those things." Condon, supposedly brilliant in his career fighting crime, makes rudimentary mistakes. The prose exhibits the lack of density common to novelizations. We never see the thoughts of the characters and even the physical backgrounds are sketches at best.

Leinster wrote comparatively few short mystery stories and they are generally unconventional. "The Gallery Gods" involves a murderer who traveled to a country without extradition agreements with the United States. He is puzzled when there is no word of the death of his victim and finally ventures out of his safe haven to find out what happened. It is, of course, a ruse to achieve just that and he is arrested. "Uneasy Home-coming" is a suspenseful story about a woman who returns after a time away from home to discover that a burglar has been using it as his headquarters, and that he is aware that she has suddenly returned. She is able to avoid death at his hands and he is captured.

In "Terror" a woman is dropped off at a remote cabin to prepare it for some visitors. Jane is expecting to be joined shortly by George Holloway, an acquaintance about whom she has recently had a vague sense of wrongness. The cabin, however, has been recently entered by parties unknown, as proven by some spilled water. A strange man comes to the front door, muttering almost unintelligibly about a telephone message, then disappears when she refuses to let him in. He breaks a window and chases her with an axe. She swims out into the nearby lake and he follows in a rowboat, but does not find her. Jane watches as he returns to the house and discards his disguise. Not surprisingly, he is Holloway, who wanted to make certain she never told anyone that she had seen him with a woman who was later murdered. The disguise seems unnecessary since he intended to kill her. In "Night Drive" (1950) a woman agrees to give a lift to the niece of a friend along a road where two women have been murdered in the past. The niece insists that she knows who the killer is, and the driver suddenly becomes convinced that her passenger is actually a man in woman's clothing. The local gas station attendant flags them down, claiming to have had an accident. The niece reveals her true gender and identifies himself as the husband of one of the victims, hoping to lure the killer into a trap. The rest happens off stage, but it appears that the widower kills the attendant, who was faking accidents in order to get access to vulnerable drivers. In "Possessed" (1957) a small town sheriff outsmarts the psychotic killer who has captured him. "Crime Wave" is a vignette in which a policeman tricks a bank robber into revealing himself. "Two in a Boat" is about a man who outsmarts an escaping killer by sabotaging the engine of his small boat and leaving his would-be kidnapper adrift.

Leinster also wrote a series of six stories about a kind of Shadow/private detective known as the Black Bat. In "The Hollywood Murders" he is on the trail of a gang that specializes in blackmail. He and a police officer named Hines are on a train with an actress who is their latest target. Someone sends the actress a box of poisoned candy but her secretary is the one who eats it and nearly dies. It is an attempt to frame the actress for murder. After arriving in Hollywood, murder follows and this time the actress is arrested, but the Black Bat ferrets out the truth. This type of story did not play to the author's strengths and it is not surprising that he dropped the character fairly quickly.

WESTERNS

Leinster published a number of traditional western novels during the 1930s, but less than half of them were reprinted as paperbacks and one of those was a movie novelization. They appeared primarily under the Jenkins name. *Mexican Trail* (1933) was published as by Will Jenkins and was serialized as *Dead Man's Shoes*. It is somewhat uncharacteristically for the genre set in the early 20th Century. Pete Gray has been framed for the murder of a fellow member of the Border Patrol named Brandon and Neil Denham knows it and manages to help him escape jail. Gray is convinced that he was set up by a criminal known as the Boss, who traffics in drugs and other illegal activities. Gray stays mostly away from towns and manages to survive, but after a few months, he stumbles across the body of Denham, who apparently has also been trying to track down the Boss. The body has been salted with objects designed to make it look as though he was actually Pug Wilson, who works for the Boss.

Gray takes Denham's horse and a short time later meets Marcia Brandon, sister of the first murdered man, who believes that he is Neil Denham. She received a telegram saying that he was coming, but the telegram was sent after Denham was dead, so obviously an imposter is on his way. She runs a cattle ranch and there have been several incidents recently designed to implicate her ranch hands in attacks on an adjacent property managed by Tom Hope. Although Hope and Brandon are on good terms, the men on both ranches are on the verge of a major brawl.

Two men, each from one side, are found dead, apparently having killed one another. But Gray points out inconsistencies that indicate a third party, probably a group of several men, killed them both and staged things to suggest a quarrel. This goes a long way toward soothing all of the cowboys, but Hope quietly tells Gray that he has previously met Denham and knows Gray is not the same man. Gray suggests that he actually met Pug Wilson, who was impersonating Denham, confusing matters further.

The ranchers are still not entirely mollified. Someone slips Gray a note indicating that his real identity is known, which suggests that the Boss has informants working at one or both ranches. Three outlaws are captured, but then released from the jail clandestinely.

Gray is framed for their escape and has a brief confrontation with a Border Patrol man named Bell, but is able to prove that he was elsewhere at the time.

A gunman tries to ambush Gray but is killed in the ensuing gunfight. A second attempt fares no better. Gray and Brandon have become romantically linked, but that relationship runs into trouble with word of the arrival in the area of Denham's wife, who is looking for her husband. Gray is not married, of course, but Brandon still believes that he is Denham and is furious about having been tricked.

Fresh questions arise about Gray's true identity, but Denham's widow backs up his lie, apparently having decided to trust him. He leads a posse that tangles with some bandits. Gray gets framed yet again, this time for burning a barn, and is also involved in a lengthy gun duel with Bell, who claims that he thought Gray was trying to ambush him. Gray is framed a couple of more times – and rather repetitively, and the reader might wonder why no one seems to detect a pattern.

Gray finds the Boss at last and pretends that he wants to join the bandits. To do so, he must first shoot a prisoner, but the gun turns out to be loaded with blanks. Gray knew this because the prisoner could see the filed down heads of the bullets and told him by eye movements that they were safe. This scene if highly improbable.

The two men escape and Gray now knows that Bell is an imposter. His real name is Wilson and he is the master criminal. The Boss is just fronting for him. With the help of the angry ranch hands, Gray brings him to justice at last. The writing is fine but the plot depends on too many situations that are artlessly contrived.

Fighting Horse Valley (1934) also appeared as by Will Jenkins. An abridged version was published in 1949 as *Texas Gun Slinger*. The title refers to the location of the town of Alminas, where Chet Holliday decides to reopen an abandoned gold mine. Although this is a western, it also has a contemporary setting so there are gas stations and automobiles. Chet had run away from Alminas when he was fourteen. The first person he recognizes upon returning is Buck Enderby, an old friend from his rodeo days. Chet has also purchased Typhoon, a wild horse, after he became the first person to stay mounted on the animal for three minutes.

Chet briefly meets Carol Bradley, who lives with her uncle, Wallace. Chet vaguely remembers Wallace and is puzzled when the man expresses his clear and apparently unprovoked hatred. The local lawyer is Julian de Aviguez, who appears to be close to Wallace. Chet is also interested in finding the Hanks family, who took him in when he was orphaned. To his consternation, the town sheriff tells him that he is persona non grata and should move on, but refuses to provide any explanation.

Chet locates and moves in with the Hanks family, but Buck shows up to tell him Wallace is willing to pay well if he were to move on. Moments later Bradley appears as well, having been told that Chet is an ex-convict who will only bring harm to the Hanks family, whom she has been trying to help. Lisbeth Hanks, only seventeen, has an awkward crush on Chet. Her father tells him that the reason Wallace hates him is because his wife ran off with Chet's father, who was a widower. The fact that two saddles have recently been found in the hills, one of them designed for a woman, rather telegraphs the explanation. Obviously someone killed Wallace's wife and her lover and concealed their bodies in the abandoned mine.

An unknown stranger tries to ambush Chet at the mine and Chet kills him. Enderby is convinced that Wallace is not behind the attempt and suggests that he claim that the man attacked him instead of Chet and that he killed him in self defense. Wallace is more incensed than ever because Chet and Carol have fallen in love, but Chet perseveres and opens the entrance to the mine. Almost immediately he and Enderby find two skeletons, one with a knife in its back.

Enderby goes to town to tell de Aviguez and the sheriff, but they claim he never arrived. Instead the sheriff and two deputies come looking for Chet with drawn guns, but fail to find him. Lisbeth tries to poison Typhoon out of spite, so Chet moves out. Near the mine, he finds Wallace and de Aviguez. Carol shows up and defuses what might have been a gunfight.

Chet goes to town and discovers that Enderby did in fact arrive, and that he left with the lawyer and the sheriff. The sheriff tries to arrest him for the murder of Enderby but Chet gets away. He discovers that Carol has been lured off and that he is suspected of having kidnapped her as well. He suddenly remembers that he suspects the sheriff of being involved in smuggling – a rather clumsy authorial artifice – and telephones him pretending to be a courier needing a guide to de Aviguez.

Believing that Carol is dead, Chet sets Typhoon lose, then forces the sheriff to lead him to what he hopes is de Aviguez's hideout. It is a trap, however, and Chet is shot. The killer is then stomped to death by Typhoon, who has not run off after all. Wallace shows up and is captured. With the help of two boys he helped escape from jail, Chet takes the sheriff and Wallace with him to de Aviguez's real hideout, where they find him gloating over Carol and Enderby, who are both still alive. They overhear him confessing to having raped and murdered Wallace's wife, then killing Chet's father to make it look like they ran off together.

In a rather rushed ending, they rescue the twosome and capture de Aviguez. Wallace then uses dynamite to kill himself and the lawyer. It is never really explained why Wallace was so determined that the mine not be reopened. Otherwise, this was a quite presentable western adventure with a touch of murder mystery thrown in.

Outlaw Sheriff (1934, aka *Rustlin' Sheriff*) is more traditional, but not nearly as well done. Dave Gilmore left his younger brother Ted in charge of their ranch while he went off to see the world. When he returns, he hears rumors that Ted is running a rustling operation, so he pre-emptively tells the local sheriff that he, Dave, is the rustler, even though he believes the charge is a lie.

Obviously he has to leave the area, but in doing so he observes a gunfight and helps a man named Tate, who hints that he is involved in something crooked and a lot more profitable than simple rustling. Since Dave is now a wanted man, he gets recruited to fight on one side in a range war between two large ranches. Martha Joyce is the niece of the man on one side of the fight, and she is trying to find a peaceful solution to the conflict, but the menfolk are not amenable. Dave also meets the head of the other faction, Grady, who is irascible but seems honest.

He visits the nearby town where Sheriff Kinley makes him a deputy, even though he believes that Dave is a rustler. He orders Dave to arrest Grady, which suggests that he is being paid by or is frightened by Martha's uncle. Some of Joyce's cattle are planted on Grady's ranch, but he discovers what is going on. Joyce and the sheriff assumed that Grady would either kill Dave and become an outlaw, or would agree to the arrest and would be in their power, and when Dave tells them instead that Grady did not steal the cattle, that they are being returned, and that he is on his way in to talk to the sheriff, Joyce walks off in a huff. The sheriff hints that he might fire Dave, who politely delivers a veiled threat about what might happen if he did so.

Dave appoints himself sheriff after overhearing Kinley and Joyce plan an ambush and a stampede and passing that information to Grady. Joyce hires another man to kill Dave but that plan fails as well. Dave gets a letter from his brother in which he brags about his career as a rustler, much to Dave's dismay. Martha discovers that her uncle is buying rustled cattle and that he has hired people to kill Dave. She decides to do something about it since the ranch is legally hers.

Joyce has Martha locked up and plans to kill Dave, but Tate takes that moment to demand money to keep silent about some secret that has not yet been revealed. Dave escapes in the confusion and goes to Grady, who is reluctant to believe him. He sneaks back onto the Joyce ranch to rescue Martha and a gunfight follows. Grady and his men show up and they manage to get away in the confusion but Dave is wounded.

The next day they run into Tate, who is trying to leave the area because Joyce now wants him dead as well. Grady has been captured and is currently locked up in the jail, but Joyce plans to have him killed in a fake escape attempt. Dave and Martha take over the jail but do not free Grady. Brother Ted shows up and a bitter argument follows.

Dave locks up his brother and releases Grady, who now believes his story. Grady brings more men to town in time to capture Joyce before he can kill anyone else. Martha and Grady convince Ted to change his name and leave the country so that his brother will not have to send him to prison. The awkward romance between Martha and Dave appears headed toward marriage. Tate's secret was that he found oil while he was prospecting for water.

The plot is less than convincing at times. Dave never even talks to his brother before claiming that he was a rustler, and we later discover that he never believed his brother was guilty – although he was – so his confession does not make sense. Some of the later developments are heavily dependent upon coincidence.

Kid Deputy (1935) is also a coming of age story. The Kid, who is never named, rides into a remote valley looking for his friend the sheriff, who disappeared four days earlier. Armed men try to keep him out but he outsmarts them. Then he encounters Joan Garland, who had hoped he was bringing a posse to rescue her and the sheriff. She hints that rival gangs dominate the valley and tells him to hide, and shortly thereafter he discovers that groups of men are searching for him.

The Kid finds the sheriff's horse and assumes its owner is dead. The gangs are split between two dominant men named Haney and Blagby. The Kid comes to the assistance of a man beset by bandits and learns some of what is happening in the valley. After some minor adventures, The Kid confronts Haney and we learn that he is Haney's son. Various mostly rather dull encounters follow before The Kid saves Joan and clears the valley of outlaws. This was probably Leinster's least successful western novel, dull, awkwardly written, and repetitive.

Black Sheep (1936) is the story of Steve Galt, who is returning to his family home after years of absence because of something he did when he was younger which is only gradually revealed as the story progresses. Even as a young boy he had realized that his uncle was a tyrant and that some of the ranch hands were rustling on the side. Steve had never been able to control his temper and had made it obvious how he felt about things, which resulted in a blackening of his reputation. Eventually he was framed for rustling himself to prevent him from telling the authorities.

Approaching the family ranch, he hears gunshots, then encounters a lone rider who forces him to surrender his boots, although oddly enough the stranger pays for them. Then he finds a dead man named Harrison, an old friend of his father, shot multiple times and assumes the thief was responsible.

Steve knows that his Uncle Peter is crooked and warns his cousin, Oliver, to warn his father off. The ranch belongs to Peter for as long as he lives, but upon his death it reverts to Steve, who is impatient for the chance to fire the foreman, Swain. But predictably his path forward becomes troubled when he comes under suspicion for the murder of Harrison.

Steve convinces Harrison's daughter Lucy that he did not kill her father. An informal posse almost captures and hangs him but he escapes. A deputy stumbles upon the rustling operation and is killed, and that murder is also blamed on Steve. He is eventually arrested, but the sheriff is not convinced that he is guilty and intends to resist attempts by a mob to lynch him. Subsequent events bear out Steve's story and the sheriff becomes convinced that Steve did not kill the deputy. He deputizes him in the dead man's place, but the sheriff himself is killed only a few minutes later so the respite is a very short one.

After escaping the mob, Steve rides to the Harrison ranch, worried that Lucy might be killed or kidnapped to gain control of her cattle. Oliver is visiting and he and the Harrison foreman form an uneasy alliance when a party of men begin sneaking up on the house. They drive them off and try to track down Swain, which leads to a gunfight in which Oliver is fatally wounded. He admits that he was the one who killed Harrison, and that he had been involved with the rustling but was sick of it.

Swain captures Lucy and disappears. A mob appears and Steve talks them out of killing him and recruits some into a posse. They return to the Galt ranch where Steve eventually kills Swain and rescues Lucy. It turns out that his uncle has actually been dead for a year, with Oliver covering it up, so the ranch is his. Some of the dialogue is very awkward and the story is all too familiar, but that is a common problem in the western genre because of the small number of plots available.

Dallas (1950) was a novelization of the screenplay by John Twist. Blayde Hollister was a Confederate officer stunned by the end of the war. He returns to his home in Georgia to find it has been burned to the ground. His family was wiped out by a band of outlaws called the Marlow gang who exploited the chaos after the surrender. Following an encounter with a belligerent Union officer, Hollister turns outlaw, but his primary concern is to track down and kill the Marlows.

Hollister had publicly offered a substantial reward for information about the Marlows. One of their friends tries to kill him and another group of men do the same, hoping to take the money from his body. He makes friends with Wild Bill Hickok, who talks him into faking his own death to throw off further pursuit. An inexperienced new marshal named Martin Weatherby stumbles onto the truth and has to be kept incommunicado until he can be convinced that he should not reveal the truth and place an innocent man in jeopardy.

21

Weatherby not only decides to accompany Hollister on his quest, he allows him to adopt his identity as a marshal. The two of them successfully intervene against a gang raiding a small town. They continue on their way afterward and eventually teach Texas. Weatherby had intended to go there originally because of his affection for Antonia Robles, so he welcomes that decision. Her family owns a large ranch in an area that is currently troubled by rustlers.

They are welcomed by Antonia's father, although only she knows which one of them is really Weatherby. Her brother Luis is also bitter about the outcome of the war. William Marlow is in the area, pretending to be a banker who has broken with his outlaw brothers. Hollister confronts him, tells him that he knows his brothers are working for him, and he is promptly attacked again. This time he kills Cullen Marlow. Hollister also locates Bryant's hideout but is unable to kill him.

Predictably, Antonia transfers her affection to Hollister. Will Marlow campaigns to be mayor of Dallas and talks about an obviously bogus plan to form a posse and track down his brother. One of the townspeople recognizes Hollister as a Confederate officer and he worries that his background will emerge. Hollister eventually kills Bryant, then defends the Robles home from an armed attack by the gang. William Marlow also dies during the battle. Hollister and Antonia become engaged and Hollister receives an official pardon for his past crimes.

There is clear sympathy for the Confederacy throughout the novel. Leinster was from Virginia. The injustices of the occupation and the venial nature of most Union officers is emphasized, but there is no mention of the fact that the Confederates were essentially traitors or that they were fighting to defend slavery. The Marlows, incidentally, are William, Cullen, and Bryant, an allusion to the famous poet.

Outlaw Guns (1950, aka *Wanted! Dead or Alive!*) is another story set relatively late for a western – there are automobiles. Slim Galway is told that his brother Buck was killed by a posse while found changing brands on cattle. The reader, as well as Galway, knows that this is not true. A local rancher is buying out the smaller ones and the sheriff is in his pocket. Buck was killed in an ambush in an effort to seize control of his ranch.

Galway returns from Africa determined to discover the truth and get justice for his brother. On the train from the east, Galway meets a man who looks a little like him. Both of them have noticed a third, who has been watching them clandestinely. Galways disarms the man and finds a telegram from Sheriff Getty which suggests that Galway should be killed before he leaves the train. The gunman finds another weapon and Galway is forced to kill him. The assassin's body falls off the train so no one else knows about it. He suspects that the man resembling him was supposed to take his place.

When the train arrives, Galway overhears two men who believe that the killer's absence means that he succeeded in his mission. He quietly begins to follow the twosome but then decides to talk to the local banker, Fulton, instead. Fulton believes the story about his brother's death, but he also notes that Getty is a terrible sheriff, that everyone is in fear of their life, and that a squatter named Hank Pace is openly raiding the local ranches. He also learns that another rancher was killed along with his brother and that the latter's niece, Benny Howe, is trying to hold onto that ranch.

Galway notices some eastern gangsters in town just before another attempt is made to kill him. He takes refuge at the Howe ranch and tells Benny Howe that he believes her uncle and his brother were murdered. He escapes yet another ambush after learning that someone is indeed impersonating him. A ranch hand is murdered at the Howe ranch and Galway is described, but not named, in a wanted poster. Benny Howe appears to have disappeared and may have been kidnapped.

Galway finds Hank Pace and his two sons, who are not very good outlaws, and they follow his lead. They rescue Howe and one of the Easterners deserts and joins them. They break another friend out of jail before he can be murdered while "escaping." Later they watch in shock as one of the gangsters uses a machine gun to kill all eight men in the posse that is searching for them because they stumbled upon a secret chemical laboratory.

There is a good deal more running and fighting before Galway starts to piece the puzzle together. Fulton has been working with men producing illegal drugs and selling them. Galway kills Fulton and is fighting with the rest of the gang when federal narcotics agents show up, having been contacted by Benny Howe. Getty is exposed as a crook. Galway proposes to Howe. Competently told but most of it is very familiar.

Son of the Flying 'Y' (1951) was Leinster's final western novel. Bud Hornaby is the son of a rancher who does not trust him to run things in his absence. So when King Hornaby leaves on an extended trip, the foreman – Budy's uncle - is put in charge. Unfortunately, the following day a stranger shows up and Uncle Paul admits that the man has a valid grudge against him. The stranger, Clem Short, kills him in a fair gunfight. Bud tries to challenge Short, even though he is hopelessly outclassed, but is tricked into delaying while Short leaves town.

After that, Bud finds himself being nursemaided by the new foreman, Joe Bradley. Bud decides to set out on his own and track down Short, sneaking away to do so. Inexperienced, he gets into trouble with a prostitute and a drifter named Chuck Brady. Brady teaches him the basics of fighting with his fists. They spend some time with a small time rancher, Jasper Knowlton, and his daughter Janet. Knowlton's brother-in-law turns out to be Clem Short. Brady pretends to be Bud to confuse pursuers.

They run into a group of friendly but devious Apaches and Bud inadvertently engineers a situation that has a happy ending for both parties. The Knowltons find out about the feud with Short and try to convince him to drop the matter, but he considers it a matter of honor, even though it appears that Short is an admirable man.

Bradley shows up and tries to take Bud back to the ranch by force but the Knowltons take the younger man's side. A crooked lawman locks him up but Bud engineers a jail break with two other men. Later he runs into his father and reluctantly surrenders his guns. King Hornaby wrongly believes that the Knowltons are rustlers because of Bradley's lies. Bradley, it turns out, is behind the rustling and Bud learns the truth. Bradley and his men realize they are in trouble and become desperate. Bradley shoots King Hornaby, not fatally, but Bud kills the outlaw after a major gunfight in town. He resolves his differences with Clem Short and ends up with Janet.

Most of Leinster's westerns are coming of age stories, and this is no exception. Bud Hornaby is perhaps the best drawn protagonist in any of the westerns, and his evolving attitude is the heart of the story. The western was already declining in popularity at this point and Leinster abandoned it for other genres.

ADVENTURE

Leinster began writing during the early days of the pulp magazines, a large number of which were adventure oriented. He was very successful, particularly with contemporary but exotic settings, and many of these stories are quite readable today. One of Leinster's earliest adventure stories was "Grooves," in which a gang of Mexican revolutionaries holds a woman hostage during a raid across the border. The title refers to the tendency to think along predictable patterns. The protagonist outwits the bandits because he is left handed and therefore takes her captor by surprise. "Footprints in the Snow" is an offbeat tale that appears to be about a genuine werewolf until the rationalized conclusion. A dead man was found in his cabin but even though the footprints indicate that only a single woman approached the cabin, his throat was torn out by what was obviously a wolf. The explanation is that the woman carried a maimed wolf to take the life of the man who had mistreated the wolf and raped the woman.

There were three stories about Malay Collins, a master thief headquartered in what was then called the Orient, all published in 1930. "The Eye of Black A'Wang" introduced Collins, who is intent upon stealing a fabled ruby from a primitive temple. His partner makes the first attempt and dies when a trap drops him into a nest of snakes, but Collins has noticed that the jewel is a fake and that the real one is elsewhere in the temple, so his follow up is a success.

Collins returned in "The Emerald Buddha." The title refers to a statue carved from a single emerald that is kept in a guarded building in Siam. Collins is summoned by a local priest who tells him that the figure is a fake and that he possesses the real one, which was stolen some years earlier. He wants Collins to surreptitiously replace the fake with the genuine jewel so that the worshippers will not know that it has been missing. Collins succeeds, but discovers that he has been duped, so he leaves the real one and brings back the fake to expose the conspiracy.

The final story is "The Black Stone of Agharti." Collins is hired to steal an artifact before its presence precipitates a major war. Previous attempts to steal it have failed because the identity of the thieves was somehow always known in advance. On his way Collins realizes that there are spies among his companions, and while one of them dies after revealing his treachery, there is at least one more. Collins unmasks the other one before arriving at his destination and the story ends with his having approached successfully, though he has not yet stolen, the Black Stone. All three stories are fair adventures, tinged with some unfortunate but inevitable contemporary racism.

"Juju" is a novella set in West Africa. The narrator is the leader of a caravan who is surprised when a plantation owner named Evan Graham – whose native help are essentially his slaves – allows a witch doctor to perform a ceremony in their village. A few weeks later he is talked into providing escort service for two women who wish to visit the plantation. When he arrives, Graham's brother Arthur is there. He recently shot a female gorilla and the male has been following him for several days, killing his bearers when it has a chance. One of the women, Alicia, is engaged to Arthur and the other is their cousin.

The following day all of the bearers and all but one of the servants have disappeared. The native village is deserted but they can hear drums in the distance. The gorilla is prowling around so they stay inside, but the following morning the remaining servant girl is found with a broken neck. They assume it was the gorilla until they realize that there is no sign of forced entry.

They photograph the dead woman's eyes because supposedly the last things a person sees remains on the retina, a bizarre superstition that shows up in several stories from this period. This confirms that a gorilla was responsible. There are no tracks leading away from the house so they assume the gorilla is still inside, but a thorough search fails to find anything out of place. After a dog is killed, the gorilla is spotted on the roof, but it somehow disappears again.

That night, they notice a figure approaching and shoot it, but it is the witch doctor and not the gorilla. The dying man admits that he was going to put a juju spell on them and that the natives were going to attack in force the following morning and kill all of the outsiders. The siege gets underway but the gorilla mauls some of the natives and that destroys the momentum of their attack.

The conclusion is startling. Arthur is killed, apparently by the gorilla, but the narrator discovers that Evan is responsible, using a gorilla suit that he also employed to keep the natives quiescent. He assumes that the vengeful gorilla has already died. The recent uprising resulted from a slip in his control that he hopes to restore. Arthur's death means that the family fortune will go to Evan so it was convenient to include that in his agenda. His plans go awry, however, as the real gorilla shows up and kills him. This is a very good story, one of Leinster's best non-SF tales.

In "Nerve" a man who parachutes out of hot air balloons quits after surviving a near fatal accident. "Stories of the Hungry Country" concerns the wife of the governor of a Portuguese colony who decides to do something about the rampant slavery, much to the dismay of her husband. Her attitude changes when an attempt is made to poison her. This story is sharply critical of "contract labor" as a disguise for what is in reality slavery.

In "The Seventh Bullet" an uneducated and disreputable man is hired to kill an unpopular Raja. He is superstitious and performs a ritual which he believes means that six of his seven bullets will magically hit their target, while the seventh and last is reserved for the use of Satan. His first bullet kills the Raja despite an illusion designed to protect him. The second kills the man who hired the killer and who hoped to silence him to cover his own involvement. The third cuts down a man who started to raise an alarm when he saw the killer fleeing. The other three are expended during his flight and when he is trapped in the jungle and facing death by torture, he decides to use the seventh bullet on himself. And it is a dud.

"The Man Who Went Black" is an account of a man on the run from cannibals in the Solomon Islands who forces a renegade white man to help him escape. "Rose O' Sharon" is a mild adventure set in Algeria that explains why a local aristocrat is indebted to a mangy camel. "Island Honor" is a rather minor tale of a tyrannical local government agent whose assassination is covered up by a doctor sympathetic to the local people.

"The Red Stone" opens with three people marooned on a small island. One is a fugitive murderer who would just as soon not be rescued. One is a police detective with a broken arm and no weapon who wants to bring him to justice. The third is a young woman with no connection to either of the others, and no desire to be raped. A duel of wits ensues which is complicated by the discovery of a red stone mounted on a statue, which may or may not be a giant ruby. There is a nice twist at the end as we discover it is actually a piece of evidence that the detective was carrying and employed as a ruse, and is not valuable at all.

"Sharks" is an excellent story about three ships and crews harvesting oyster shells and pearls. None of them like any of the others and when a crew member on one ship disappears along with all their accumulated pearls, it is assumed that he joined one of the other ships, which mysteriously departed at just the right moment. But things are not what they appear. When one of the owners begins to object strenuously when his partner tries to do some shark fishing, it is only a matter of time until it is discovered that he killed the man and threw him to the sharks so that the wrong person would be suspected.

"The Man Who Didn't Shoot" is quite short. Two men who stole a ruby from an idol have a falling out. They both die but the better of the two accomplishes his purpose because the ruby is concealed inside the revolver he did not use to defend himself, which is forwarded to his family after his death.

"The Trail of Blood" is a novelette set in Angola. A halfbreed named Nguki has established a small empire that blocks an important trading route. An Englishman named Wellington attempts to secure a promise not to raid into British held territory, but Nguki wants a white queen. Well armed with Portuguese guns, he lays siege to the fort where Wellington is stationed, then sends a party to capture the staff of a mission station deeper in British territory, which includes people of both genders.

Nguki's party captures one woman and kills everyone else. Wellington has started a rumor of a large British force in the area, so the raiders plan a circuitous return to their own territory. There are a thousand of them and Wellington has only eight native soldiers with him, so he sets up a series of harassing raids that significantly diminishes the number of men available to Nguki. Further efforts to suggest a large punitive force is in the area cause Nguki to split his forces and race for home with only thirty men and his captive. More tricks follow and he is finally captured and sent to be hanged. This is another of Leinster's best non-science fiction stories.

"Tuilagi" is rather minor. An old feud gets resolved thanks to some headhunters. In "Jungle Stream" two men waiting on a Brazilian river to ambush the cousin of one of them fall prey to a tribe using poisoned blowgun darts. "According to the Directory" is another tale of deceit. There is supposed to be a small treasure on a deserted island that has been overrun by poisonous spiders, but the spiders do not exist and it is a clever double-doublecross on the part of two unscrupulous men.

"The God Who Carried a Cane" is another story of pearl diving. The protagonist, Kennedy, is driven onto an island by a storm and is taken prisoner. Another white man has been posing as a prophet and has gathered a large number of pearls. His partner is supposed to return by ship to take him and the pearls away, but he expected to be double crossed so he set a trap by preparing the natives to believe he is evil. Unfortunately, Kennedy has triggered the trap and is scheduled to be killed in the other man's place. As it happens, however, he speaks the local language and he is able to convince the villagers that he is a demon who will be freed from his bonds if they do him any harm. A rain storm loosens the ropes and Kennedy is able to kill the false prophet, secure the pearls, and escape on his own boat.

"The Village of the Devil-Devil Drums" is a relatively minor story about a fugitive trapped on an island of head hunters who pretends to be a god and kills the local witch doctor. "Gun Cargo" is a novelette set in Sumatra. Frederick Denny overhears some members of the crew of a ship where he is working as they talk about a local bandit with whom they sometimes cooperate. The ship's captain forcibly sends him ashore where other bandits try to kill him before he can reveal that the two groups plan to attack the town while its soldiers are elsewhere. It is puzzling in these circumstances why the mutineers, who are in league with the bandits and in fact are bringing him a shipment of weapons, did not simply kill Denny.

Denny joins forces with a young Dutch businessman and a Chinese Christian boy in an effort to rescue a young woman presumed to be held hostage by the bandits. They arrive at the outpost and discover that they have reached it before the bandits, but only by a short amount of time. Denny's former ship is anchored there and he organizes an attack that successfully seizes control. Unfortunately the ship goes aground on a mud bank. The bandits arrive and prevent them from returning to the shore, but they are also unable to reach the ship. Skirmishes ensue. The Chinese boy is sent clandestinely to the mainland to try to alert the authorities and bring soldiers to the rescue. The army, however, is not strong enough to take offensive action so eventually Denny and the others find a way to free the ship and steam away to freedom.

"Payung" is a slow moving story of a trader who is so malleable that he is convinced to help foment a rebellion he does not believe in. "Maehoe" is a houseboy who gets involved with Gleason, a nefarious man who has gained the enmity of a local chieftain after an unsuccessful attempt at theft. Circumstances eventually lead to Gleason's capture after he betrays the people trying to help him. "White-Man Devil" describes how a man imprisoned by a local witch doctor uses tribal superstitions to outwit him and escape. An exaggerated bit of bragging results in a death in "The Boast of Mat Drus."

"Side Bet" is a minor classic. The protagonist is the sole human survivor of a shipwreck, and he is left on a small, barren island where he attempts to salvage stray items from the ship that occasionally show up near shore. He is not alone, however. One of the rats from the ship also made it to safety and the two are rivals for the dwindling supply of food and drink. There is a single cask of water and a box of biscuits. They duel for a while and at the last moment the man decides the rat has won because he is too weak to go on. And at that moment, he is rescued, but he insists upon leaving a cache of food for the rat since it won the bet.

"A Night to Survive" concerns a pilot who is forced to bail out of his plan over a remote island whose inhabitants are likely to be hostile. He has a broken ankle and an injured arm, and only a pistol with which to defend himself. But there is a dog on the island which once belonged to a trader and which rightly fears the local people. With the dog's assistance, he repels three attempts to murder him before a rescue party arrives and takes both him and the dog to safety.

"Beautiful Widow" is a pirate story. Captain Morgan has been captured by the Spanish and is to be hanged. He manages a fairly clever escape and then meets the young wife of an aristocrat held prisoner by his crew. He refuses the ransom and tells her the man is dead to spare her having to spend the rest of her life with her unpleasant husband and then orders the prisoner to be hanged. "Insult to the Family" is set in a Latin American country whose government is facing increasing unrest. A pair of elderly women decide to uphold the family honor despite the violence around them and end up manipulating the fate of their country.

"No Road Too Hard" has an element of adventure but it is mostly about a man who forges a bond with his stepson. The boy has secretly bought a wrecked car and restored it so that he can be the first to drive to the top of a nearby mountain. The stepfather figures out the secret and it reminds him of a similarly foolish but spectacular event from his own youth, and that allows him to find common ground at last. "Between Moves" involves a rescue at sea during a storm.

ROMANCE

Jenkins wrote some short romance fiction as Louisa Carter Lee and used that name for three books, *Her Desert Lover* (1925), *Her Other Husband* (1929), and *Love and Better* (1931). They are not very memorable and only the first is relatively available.

Her Desert Lover – which is a mystery as well as a romance - has a male protagonist, Philip Lane. He and his sister Laura find an unknown young woman wandering in a storm and bring her into the house they share. Philip has just returned from a long stay in the Middle East. They put the stranger up for the night and in the morning, though she is otherwise recovered, she tells them that she remembers nothing, not even her name. There is no evidence of any physical injury.

The body of a second woman is found near the house a short time later. Although it is clear that she has been murdered, Lane has her body taken into the house before calling the police. Ellen Kenwood, Philip's rather obstreperous aunt, promptly shows up. She identifies the dead woman as Daisy Kenyon, her sister, who was disowned by their father. They also discuss the history of a nearby house, apparently owned by a wealthy older man who was later replaced by a younger one, presumably having died and willed it to the newcomer. Neither was particularly sociable.

The mystery woman leaves without telling them where she is going, and the local authorities begin to suspect her of having committed the murder. Philip tracks her down and discovers that her memory has returned, although she still refuses to tell him her real name. She insists that her father is trying to force her into a marriage she does not desire and he assures her that he will protect her.

Harold Davis is the prospective suitor, and he is painted as a villain as soon as he appears. Apparently he has some leverage against the father of Beatrice Hale, the mystery woman, and he is angry when he discovers that she has been seen in the company of another man. Beatrice returns to the Lane house, but Ellen Kenwood turns her over to Davis. He and her father take her to a remote cottage where she is held prisoner.

Beatrice hears a conversation that indicates that her father and Davis were involved in something illegal, and also that Davis is not really her father. Lane's aunt lies and tells him that Beatrice left voluntarily. Daisy Kenwood had at one time been married to Davis under another name.

Beatrice is indicted for murder, despite the lack of any real evidence and her lack of a motive, but she remains a captive. Philip confronts Davis and the two men have a public brawl. The police show up at the house to arrest Beatrice but Philip sneaks her away in the confusion. At the last minute a witness turns up who saw the murder and Davis is identified formally as the killer and arrested. The mystery is rather transparent and the romance quite low key, though the story is reasonably well told.

"The Street of Magnificent Dreams" is a short and very minor romance. A man who has never been much of a success has helped a number of other people achieve their life ambitions and his wife finally tells him that this makes him the most successful of them all. Leinster was never very good at portraying deeply emotional situations and he wrote very little in this genre.

"Persian Love Story" is much better. A child bride in Iran grows to adolescence during World War II and through happenstance is thrust into the company of a handsome American for two days, which would be fatal to her reputation as a wife regardless of what actually happened. The husband pretends to be understanding but the American disappears and is never seen again. The war ends and the husband is so badly injured that he longs for death, but his wife refuses to let him die, and finally admits that she knows he paid for the murder of the man she loved.

"The Man Who Lived Alone" is quite moving. A minor French official working in the South Pacific sacrifices his career to marry a local woman. They live together for some time before he announces that she has run off with another man. Many years pass and he continues to live in their house, growing increasingly feeble, and eventually he kills himself. When others enter the house, they discover the body of his wife, who has recently died, and who never left at all but instead contract leprosy. The husband took care of her for years in secret so that she would not have to be moved to an isolated leper colony.

SCIENCE FICTION NOVELS

Leinster's first science fiction novel was *Murder Madness* (1930), which was packaged as a mystery in book form. Charley Bell is an American secret agent who has been mysteriously ordered to South America with no idea what his mission might be. Aboard ship, he attempts to meet secretly with a member of the crew who had signaled that he is similarly under cover, but before he can do so he is confronted by Paula Canalejas, daughter of a Brazilian government official. She asks him point blank if he is a spy and he protests that he is simply a bureaucrat at the State Department. His contact tells him that he is supposed to meet with the older Canalejas who has information about the disappearance of seven agents in South America in recent weeks. An eighth agent has been rendered hopelessly insane by unknown means. Also aboard the ship is Ortiz, an ex-Argentinean government official, who seems unnaturally distressed for no discernible reason.

Ortiz tells Bell that he has been given a poison that will soon turn him into a homicidal madman. The antidote is being carried to the ship by a small seaplane but the fog is so thick that they cannot land. Ortiz refers to the Master as the one who tried to force him to commit treason or lose his sanity. An attempt to drop the antidote onto the ship fails and Ortiz shoots himself. Before dying, he tells Bell that the Master's agent in Rio de Janeiro is named Ribiera.

Bell identifies and develops a relationship with Ribiera, but Leinster simply jumps forward in time to a point where all of this has been accomplished. Bell believes that his true purpose for being in Brazil has been guessed and he escapes an attempt to subject him to a hypnotic drug. Ribiera questions him when he pretends to have succumbed. In the days that follow, Bell notices that many powerful people are clearly frightened of Ribiera.

Ribiera eventually invites Bell to his mansion and tells him that he knows about his pretense of having been drugged. Bell is now his prisoner and is pressured to voluntarily join the cause of the Master, whom Ribiera refers to as his uncle. One of the servants is ordered to seduce him and she tells Bell that they have all been drugged and must have the antidote every two weeks or they lose control of their bodies and become enraged killers.

Bell escapes in a small plane with the help of Canalejas, who tells him that he has also been poisoned and that he plans to take his own life. His daughter has been entrusted with all the information that he has gathered about the Master. They rendezvous and she passes Bell a packet of documents, but she was followed by agents of the Master who suspected her intentions. Bell manages to escape but Paula is abducted.

Having sent the documents to his superiors via another agent, Bell considers himself temporarily free of all orders and decides to rescue Paula. He returns to Ribiera's house and − through a completely implausible subterfuge − manages to remain armed long enough to take his host prisoner. Bell and Paula leave in a seaplane but are faced with a problem. Ribiera will certainly have them charged with her father's murder and the United States government would probably honor a request for extradition. Their only chance is to track down the Master and eliminate him pre-emptively and decapitate his organization.

They crash in the jungle where, rather fortuitously, they overhear radio transmissions conveying orders from the Master to his agents, all broadcast in the clear and directed to a receiver less than six miles away. Bell builds a raft and they go in search of the Master's local agents. They find a small installation, Bell kills four men off stage, and they steal another small airplane.

Bell knows that Ribiera is on his way to report to the Master, so he locates and follows his plane. The story begins to disintegrate at this point, with Bell assisted by one coincidence after another. Bell somehow calculates where the Master would have his headquarters, on a high plateau that is strategically located, based on no evidence whatsoever. They land there and Paula tells him that her uncle owns property in the area. She locates her cousin, who admits that his entire family has been enslaved by the Master. He disables their airplane before Bell realizes the danger and confesses that he is acting under compulsion and that Ribiera knows they are somewhere nearby.

They make repairs and take to the air again, eluding some pursuit planes, but eventually have to ditch their failing aircraft in another stretch of jungle. They fake a fiery crash so that Ribiera will assume that they are dead. There is another absurd coincidence as they stumble over the body of a dead American secret agent in the jungle, and find a detailed report he was carrying that provides more information about the Master. Then they steal yet another airplane and take off again.

Bell and Paula improvise petrol bombs and drop them on an airfield controlled by the Master. Unfortunately their engine dies and they are forced to resort to parachutes. Time for another coincidence. They find another secret agent locked in a cage, but he is unguarded and easily set free. Bell tells the local people that he is working for the Master and convinces them to provide a boat by which he and Paula can go to Paraguay. The freed agent has been poisoned and remains behind. Their luck runs out however. Paula is captured through some bad luck and Bell then voluntarily turns himself over to Ribiera's men.

Ortiz's son is working for the Master under duress and he decides to help the two of them escape. They join forces with yet another agent and plot the deaths of Ribiera and the Master. Unfortunately they are outwitted and Paula is taken captive once again. They finally meet the Master, who announces that Paula and Bell are free to leave, although he believes that Bell has now been infected with the poison and has only a single dose of the antidote to delay its effect. But Bell was faking the early effects of the drug and is free to act on his own.

Bell kills Ribiera and the threesome take the Master prisoner, spiriting him away on one of his own aircraft. He tells them that the drug he is using actually can enhance human intelligence, but Bell realizes that the Master is himself addicted to it. He deprives him of his supply until the secret of the antidote is revealed and the world is therefore safe from any abuse of the drug in the future. The climax is very abrupt and not very convincing.

Although this was serialized in a science fiction magazine, it only marginally falls within that genre. It is generally well written and is not dissimilar to contemporary thrillers in its overall effect. The use of a slow acting poison to compel obedience is quite possible and it is never really explained how the Master could virtually gain control over most of South America using a method that is available to every other similarly inclined villain. The frequency of coincidences is really embarrassing, however, and as a whole it is not a particularly good story.

The Murder of the U.S.A. (1946, aka *Destroy the U.S.A.)* opens with a nuclear attack that effectively wipes out the country's military and infrastructure, destroying every major city. One third of the population dies in the first few minutes and no counterattack was launched because the identity of the aggressor nation is unknown. This premise appeared in more than one story during this era, although it would soon become almost a given that the Soviet Union was the villain.

Sam Burton is a lieutenant serving in one of a handful of military bunkers that have survived the attack. The commanding officer is Major Fred Thale. They are concerned about three unknown individuals moving on the surface above them, who might be spies searching for their location so that a bomb can be dropped. The threesome, two men and a woman, are brought inside for questioning. Burton knows the woman – Betty Clark - and announces immediately that there is overwhelming evidence that she is a spy, although he does not present any. The woman tells them that they saw some suspicious people in the area but that they were on an innocent hike when the bombs started to fall.

Elsewhere all the countries of the world search for the perpetrator, which has to be one of their number. The scenario for the attack is horribly dated, of course, and probably was not plausible even during the 1940s. Two bombs are aimed at their bunker but both are intercepted. Another party of military personnel are rescued, but Thale is unwilling to relinquish command to one of them even though he is technically his superior. The officer in question insists that he knows Clark is a spy, but another officer counters that she has actually been working for counter intelligence.

Thale is revealed to be a fifth columnist. He commits suicide when discovered, which leaves Burton in command. From certain physical evidence recovered from one of the captured spies, and other clues harvested from unexploded bombs, scientists are able to determine which country launched the attack and the rest of the world combines to annihilate it. The country is never named.

Despite the melodramatic subject matter, this is a rather dull story. Much of it consists of efforts to intercept incoming bombs or otherwise deal with the ongoing attack, and there are efforts to explain the methods in scientific or engineering detail. There are even footnotes. The characters are flat and they do not express any horror, sadness, or even much anger at what is happening around them. Although Leinster had by now been writing for about thirty years, his work at book length remained very crude and his plots relied heavily on coincidence and unexplained motivation, although much of his short fiction was already of superior quality. Many of the magazines for which he wrote did not require much sophistication from their writers, and it would have been uneconomical to spend a great deal of time polishing prose that no one would appreciate.

The Black Galaxy (1949) incorporates "The Story of Rod Cantrell." Cantrell is working on a program to explore the solar system but he opposes further voyages until an adequate weapons system can be developed. Ruins on Mars suggest that a civilization there was wiped out, perhaps by the same beings who erected an enigmatic pyramid on Calypso. Although the first three trips into space went unmolested, Cantrell worries that an inimical power is close at hand.

Cantrell clashes with politicians and is removed from his presumed captaincy of a large new spaceship, the Stellaris. This ship – we are told that this is the first actual human spaceship despite the earlier voyages – can visit any place in the galaxy. The confusion os solar systems and galaxies was quite common in early science fiction. Rod is aboard with his girlfriend, Kit Bowen, and a handful of technicians when a short circuit triggers the drive and sends them to an unknown location in space by way of a kind of hyperspace called the dark universe.

They are attacked by a pyramid shaped spaceship, but their ship is better equipped and they manage to get away. After some effort, they locate a planet. The planet has recently been attacked, perhaps because they had developed space travel and were seen as a potential rival by another race. While there, they spot a party of looters from one of the pyramid ships. Rod figures out how to use the aliens' death ray and kills the looters and the crew of three other ships before they are forced to flee into the dark universe.

The crew rather improbably finds a way to meld the alien weapons with their own so that their ship will automatically kill anything that attacks. A few alien ships do prove to be hostile and are destroyed but then a massive fleet shows up and the humans are forced back into the dark universe.

They find another ravaged planet where some of the locals

survived and evacuate them to another world. With new weaponry, they destroy an entire fleet of pyramid ships. They capture another, figure out where the aliens' home world is, and blow up their sun, effectively committing genocide. Since the home planet was broadcasting power to all of their ships in the galaxy, all of those ships are suddenly dead in space, their crews doomed. Rod and company then return to Earth.

The plot is grandiose and rather silly. There is some discussion of the morality of genocide, even in self defense, but it is superficial and comes to no conclusions. Leinster repeats here a problem found in much early science fiction, confusion about interplanetary and interstellar distances. The Stellaris is apparently capable of reaching the stars as easily as it can the nearby planets. There is even an explanation of how the drive works – it accesses another universe, but while the mechanics of this drive are not really relevant to the story the author spends a good deal of time explaining them.

The Brain-Stealers (1954, expanded from "The Man in the Iron Cap" from 1947) was Leinster's first noteworthy science fiction novel. It is set in a future where a world government suppresses scientific progress out of fear that it will lead to death and destruction – another premise that would become common in the genre in subsequent years. Jim Hunt is a scientist who has bee arrested by the security forces but who escapes from an airship, faking his own death in the process. But unbeknownst to him, that same night an alien spaceship lands nearby whose occupants can take control of human minds.

Hunt has, rather coincidentally, been experimenting with thought transmission when he had been arrested, and this makes him sensitive to the alien thoughts that permeate the area. He finds a local farm whose occupants are strangely listless. Just as he is aware that they are being manipulated by thought control, the aliens become aware of his resistance and knowledge of their power.

Hunt discovers that they are alien invaders and that each local family has one hidden in their house to control them, so he bolts. They combine their thought control into a kind of mental net to subdue him, but he uses wire to create a makeshift helmet that blocks their thoughts. Although he plans to give other helmets to the family harboring him and kill the alien they are concealing, the alarm has been given and dozens of armed and mentally controlled men begin searching for him, disrupting his plans.

He sneaks back to the farm house, disables two guards, and burns the building down, killing the resident alien. He mails a letter partially explaining the situation to the authorities, but the aliens intercept it. They organize a massive manhunt using hundreds of human slaves. Although he temporarily confuses the situation by putting a wire cap on a dying man, Hunt realizes that the aliens know that he is still free, particularly when they issue orders that no one should wear a hat.

After fashioning a wig to hide the cap, Hunt decides that his only recourse is to capture one of the aliens and bring it to a place outside the zone of control where he can prove his case to the government. He constructs a wire cage and then by means of a subterfuge manages to capture one of the aliens, who are physically quite small and physically weak. By an outrageously unlikely chance, Hunt runs into another fugitive, Miles Brandon, who is also immune to the alien thought control because of a metal plate that was placed in his head following an accident.

Hunt decides that the only answer is to find a way to reverse the process and subdue the aliens. He also thinks of a method by which the aliens could themselves completely subjugate humanity. They have now swollen to such a large number that if they should unite their thoughts, they could blanket the globe. The aliens have the same thought and the world is soon enslaved, but at the last minute Hunt is able to build a working transmitter that neutralizes their mental projections. He is forgiven for his past "crimes" and asked to help discover how to operate the aliens' spaceship so that they can be eradicated on other worlds they have conquered.

This short novel is generally well written though rather dated. Nuclear energy and other developments never happened in this context because they were outlawed during the 1950s – the story takes place in the 1970s. Jack Finney's famous *The Body Snatchers* (1955) is quite similar in structure although the aliens' mechanism of conquest is quite different. Even the titles are the same and it would not be surprising to discover that Finney was influenced by this earlier work.

Fight for Life (1947) originally appeared in magazine form as *The Laws of Chance*. The setting is shortly after an atomic war, although the author clearly had no real idea of the destructive power of atomic weapons. The atomic bomb was only two years old. Steve Sims, a former physics professor, is one of the survivors who is struggling to stay alive in a ruined landscape. He is wandering alone until he rescues a woman named Frances from a man who is attacking her. Despite his situation, Sims has been working on a paper about indeterminacy and the laws of chance.

Frances mentions that she knows a man named Lucky Connors, who also seems to have fortunate things happen to him. They run into him a short time later. Once Sims is convinced that Connors is telling the truth, he talks him into wishing for one of the still attacking aircraft to crash. Rather implausibly, no one knows who the attackers are and this is an effort to identify them, a throwback to *Murder of the USA*. Connors' luck is helped by the proximity of meteorites whose properties can be amplified mechanically. Between the two unlikely premises, it is clear that the heroes are virtually invulnerable. Or at least so it appears.

Unfortunately, the three are attacked by a horde of people who have reverted to barbarism. They survive and figure out that there are enemy agents among the survivors and that these people call in bombing runs on any group that attempts to restore order. The scale of activity required for this would be an impossible task, of course, but the novel was written during the period of postwar paranoia that saw communists everywhere.

Much of the middle section of the novel consists of experiments with the power to influence the laws of probability interspersed with threats by desperate survivors and it is rather repetitive. Sims builds weapons based on his discoveries, is able to explode falling bombs in orbit, knock planes out of the sky, and eventually he locates the enemy headquarters and threatens it with atomic explosions if the enemy soldiers fail to surrender.

The novel is rather badly done throughout. There are too many coincidences, the background is never developed enough to really give the reader a clear idea of the world situation, and the characters are poorly developed and uninteresting. Connors' abilities are essentially magic despite the efforts to rationalize his power.

The Last Space Ship (1949) is actually an assembly of three previously published short stories. The first is "The Disciplinary Circuit," which introduces Kim Rendell, citizen of the planet Alphin III in a future so distant that the galaxy is fully inhabited and matter transmission has replaced space travel. The Disciplinary Circuit is a kind of all seeing computer that can instantly locate any person on the planet and deliver increasing levels of pain. Rendell tried to develop a way to block the Circuit and has been outlawed. He cannot be given food, clothing, or shelter, although he can access the spaceship he owns, a relic of his ancestors' time, which can still be made functional. He knows that if he tries to leave by matter transmitter he will be shunted involuntarily to a prison planet so the ship is his only hope.

The Disciplinary Circuit does not actually control the government. There are several men who direct its operation and who are responsible for the various lies given to the populace while they are personally exempt from discipline. Rendell threatens to broadcast the truth from the spaceship unless Dona Brett, the woman he loves, is brought to him immediately. The council agrees, still unaware that the spaceship is functional and the two eventually escape into space.

Unfortunately, word is passed and they are forced to flee from projected beams of pain whenever they approach an inhabited world. They have limited fuel so Rendell restructures the drive so that the entire ship is a matter transmitter that does not need a receiver. Over countless centuries and countless trillions of people, no one ever thought of this particular trick before!

With this new method of travel, they visit numerous planets, only to discover that each of them is more horrible than even Alphin III. They eventually go to the prison world and convince the inhabitants there to build a new kind of matter transmitter with which they can emigrate to another galaxy and be free of the Disciplinary Circuit.

The second story in the series was "The Manless Worlds," a rather silly story. One planetary ruler has modified the pain projectors so that they kill all male humans. He uses this to leave only women and girls on a planet that he covets, then conquers it easily with conventional forces. Rendell and his friends have built a fleet of teleporting spaceships, but are unable to find the rare element needed to fuel them, and the conquering empire is headed in their direction.

Rendell constructs a fake spaceship and rigs it with a paralyzing beam. One of the empire's ships stops to investigate and its all male crew is incapacitated. That means that only Dona can go aboard safely. She steals their fuel, but a mishap when she is back on Rendell's ship propels them millions of light years across the universe. They eventually find their way back, provide fuel for the prison planet's ships, and attack the home world of the rising empire.

The final story is "The Boomerang Circuit." The interstellar matter transmitters suddenly cease to function. Word of the freedoms found on the prison planet has been circulating and it is feared that the vested interests in the first galaxy have decided to take action. Rendell uses his spaceship to investigate, finds that interplanetary warfare is on an upswing, and rescues the populace of the prison planet, which has been isolated by a gigantic force field. In the process, he discovers a way to build a device that can be dropped onto a planetary surface in order to short circuit each world's disciplinary circuit, thereby ensuring that the galaxy will be freed.

An amusing sign of the time when the stories were written is the deep concern by the two fugitives that they cannot find anyone with the authority to marry them. There is a logical flaw as well. We are told in the first part that Rendell's is the only operating spaceship in the galaxy, but the enemy empire has ships as well, and they were active before the events in part one. Rendell's ability to invent anything that he needs provides rather improbable solutions to most of his problems.

The Other Side of Here appeared in book form in 1955 but had been previously published serially as *The Incredible Invasion* in 1936. Steve Waldron is attempting to discover what happened to Erasmus Blair, a scientist, who disappeared mysteriously and without a word to his daughter Lucy. Blair was working on a theory that two objects could occupy the same space at the same time, and several of his scientific correspondents have also disappeared recently.

Blair's assistant, Fran Dutt, is wanted by the police, although Lucy insists he is innocent. They receive a phone call from him warning them that they are in danger and urging them to come to a hotel in New York. As they are driving through Newark, everyone except themselves suddenly collapses, causing multiple car wrecks and leaving the sidewalks covered with unconscious bodies. They have no idea why they have been spared and pass out of the city, whose power grid goes off a short time later, plunging them into darkness.

An examination of some of the inert bodies suggests something like petrifaction, but the authorities are reluctant to declare the victims dead. Steve and Lucy find a letter waiting for them from Dutt, which implies that he protected them from the effect of a new invention and tells her that her father is alive and well, but that he himself is in mortal danger if word gets out that he assisted them. Steve later discovers that a mysterious device had been attached to the underside of their car whose functioning he does not understand.

Steve goes to visit an expert on electrical anesthesia and is greeted by a man who closely resembles Dutt. When the stranger pulls out a weapon, Steve knocks him unconscious but not before it discharges and petrifies some laboratory mice. He returns to the hotel and confronts Dutt, who admits that he is a spy for an enemy government, but insists that he opposes the government of his nation, which readers will by now have guessed is in another reality.

The hotel and a small area surrounding it are hit by the petrification effect, but Steve and Lucy are outside the area. News reports suggest that Steve is a plague carrier, which is reinforced when other small areas where he is known to have been are subsequently affected in the same fashion. It is obviously a plot to make it impossible for them to find a safe haven. Panic snarls the streets, but the two of them are eventually able to leave Manhattan.

They reach a doctor and begin experimenting on some of the petrified mice. Steve discovers that a powerful electric current will reverse the effect and that a lesser current can prevent it from happening, which explains the device attached to their car. They decide to make their findings public so that the people affected can be restored to life. Steve also discovers that under the right conditions, the rigid tissue literally disappears, presumably into another dimension.

Their efforts to convince other doctors are discovered and result in an attack by the invaders. They leave town while the one doctor who knows the truth intends to demonstrate how to revive the victims, but he is attacked by rioters and seriously injured. The world at large now believes that Steve created the plague and is disseminating it. His efforts to reveal its true nature and its cure all fail, but he and Lucy, equipped with protective devices, enter Newark and find a large group of men looting the city and driving trucks through a giant portal back to their own world. They wear special armor which protects them from the paralyzing effect and Steve disables a guard and appropriates his armor.

Steve kills two of the leaders of the invaders, who seem to be split between aristocrats and near slaves. He then revives a scientist named Hamlin, who attempts to tell the troops guarding the cordoned area the truth, but who is fatally shot by the nervous soldiers. They revive another man but the three are thwarted in their efforts to contact the outside world. Then Dutt shows up and is taken prisoner. Steve rather implausibly convinces him that he must provoke a revolution against the aristocrats.

The invaders strike New York City next. Steve and the others manage to jury-rig something in the city's power center that temporarily reverses the effect, but it fails after a few minutes. They are surrounded by a large body of the invaders and death seems inevitable. Eventually they escape and put to sea in a small boat, where they encounter a Navy destroyer. After convincing the captain that their story is true, they build shielding devices for the crew and a counter attack drives the invaders out of the cities they have captured. Dutt, meanwhile, has led a successful revolt back in the other world and he offers peace and reparations. Although a bit clunky in spots, this has otherwise aged quite well.

Out of This World (1958) is another fix-up consisting of three short stories originally published in 1947 as by William Fitzgerald. The first of these is "The Gregory Circle" which introduces Bud Gregory, an automobile repairman in a small town who is unaware of his connection to a series of bizarre events – spontaneous cancer cures, plagues of dead animals, malfunctioning Geiger counters, etc. A scientist named David Murfree, who is disturbed by a pattern he has detected in these events, stops at Gregory's garage for repairs and discovers that the mechanic has invented some highly sophisticated devices despite having had no technical training.

A wave of mysterious mass deaths of humans and animals follows, most of them attributed to radioactive dust, although no one knows where it came from. Murfree eventually figurers out that a radical new device has run wild at a remote cabin and concludes that Gregory built something innocently that has run amuck. He forces Gregory to construct another device that will allow him to shut down the first, thereby saving the world.

"The Nameless Something" opens with an international crisis – a proliferation of nuclear weapons and another unnamed country – almost certainly Russia – threatening to launch a major attack. Gregory, meanwhile, has revamped an old car in such a way that it can travel at remarkably high speeds and stop almost instantly. The political maneuverings are impossibly naïve, and the story is more humorous than its predecessor. Spies abduct Murfree and Gregory, but the latter builds a force field device that makes their weapons useless and they escape. This same device later protects the country from a missile attack and the crisis is averted.

The third story was "The Deadly Dust." Gregory and his family are now in hiding because of the ongoing danger from foreign agents. All across the country the soil is suddenly becoming more radioactive. This time the enemy is a fleet of alien spaceships, but once again Gregory rises to the occasion and outwits them. This was the least interesting of the three stories, but they are all rather minor. The balance between humor and seriousness is not well handled. There was a fourth story in the series that was not included in the book titled "The Seven Temporary Moons," published in 1948.

Space Platform (1953) was the first volume in a near future trilogy about the construction and launching of a space station, although in this case it is to be assembled on Earth and then launched rather than put together in orbit. The protagonist is Joe Kenmore, whom we first meet as he is accompanying a crucial subassembly for a space station as it is flown to its destination. He grows increasingly nervous when the pilots tell him that sabotage by foreign powers has resulted in multiple plane crashes and other incidents, many of them fatal.

The flight is attacked by a plane firing missiles, then almost destroyed by a booby trap in the landing gear - the fire extinguishers have been filled with flammables, and one of the crates contains a bomb. The number of sabotage attempts that nearly succeed here and in the back story are rather over the top. Security would have to be incredibly lax to allow so many loopholes. The head of security is Major Holt, a friend of the Kenmore family, who is accompanied by his adult daughter Sally – who provides minimal romantic interest throughout the series but who also proves to be more intelligent than was usual in the genre at the time..

The equipment is damaged when the plan crashlands but Kenmore figures out a way to repair everything quickly. He saves a man from falling to his death and is quickly accepted by the men working at the construction site. Most of the next few chapters consist of revelations about sabotage mixed with conversations about the technical issues of building the space station and living in orbit. A few minor characters will recur in later books, but they are indistinguishable from one another.

Sally Holt was a bit unusual for a female character in this period of science fiction, although she is off stage most of the time. She is smart and assertive, handy with a firearm, and she has contributed useful technical ideas to the project which have been adopted, although it is not clear that she has any formal training in her background. She and Kenmore become romantically involved rather suddenly and awkwardly. Leinster was never comfortable with romance but usually tried to include at least a taste of it.

An attempt is made to assassinate Kenmore personally but it fails. Two of the rockets are sabotaged and Kenmore brainstorms and solves the mystery of how this was accomplished, then foils a clandestine attempt to invade the project by a group of armed men. A nuclear missile is launched from an unknown location but is destroyed by air defenses. There are arguments at the United Nations meant to convince the US to cancel the launch, which is viewed as an unacceptably shift in the balance of military power, but ultimately it is scheduled and the platform reaches space on the final page.

Although all of the characters are adults, the novel feels as though it was targeting younger readers. The plot, characterization, and writing are less sophisticated that was the case with much of the author's previous work. This may be the result of the common perception at the time that science fiction was read almost exclusively by adolescent boys. There is also a pervasive atmosphere of dread about communist agents – although not all of those opposed to the project are of that persuasion.

Kenmore returned in *Space Tug* (1953). This time he is assigned to lead a resupply mission to the orbiting space station six weeks after it was launched. Certain unnamed foreign powers are working on nuclear armed missiles to bring it down, so his cargo includes interceptor rockets. The opening chapters describing the lift off were as scientifically accurate as Leinster could make it at the time, but we know now, of course, that the process is much more elaborate than was anticipated.

They have not even arrived when they receive a message that at least one nuclear armed missile has been finished by the enemy. A short time late four rockets are launched from Earth, targeting the space platform. Kenmore and his crew rather implausibly turn their landing rockets into interceptors with proximity fuses and destroy the incoming missiles.

They reach the platform but are unable to return to Earth without their landing rockets. Sanford, the man running the platform, is singularly unpleasant and rude and tells them their situation is hopeless. He fails to explain what he means and unaccountably Kenmore does not bother to ask. Another man, Brent, explains that they have too few defensive missiles to hold out against a concerted attack. It is rather difficult to believe that the US government would not have recognized this possibility in advance and provided for it.

Kenmore suggests throwing out metallic debris to surround the station and fool the proximity fuses of any incoming missiles. Since their food is in tin cans (!) they have a considerable amount to disperse. Sanford, however, has had a psychotic break and while they are all outside, he joins them, having secured the airlock so that they cannot re-enter the station. They use some of the tin cans to focus the sunlight and burn a hole in one of the airlocks, which allows them to get back to safety with the now comatose Sanford.

Several more attacks are thwarted before a new commander named Brown arrives on a second supply ship. Both ships now return to Earth, although Kenmore's crashes after surviving another missile attack. Belatedly the government learns that the enemy nation is building a fleet of manned rockets. Kenmore comes up with a way to build spaceships fast and relatively cheaply, which might allow them to counter the threat. They also develop drone ships directed from a manned companion vessel.

Commander Brown turns out to be an almost comically inept administrator, not much more than a cartoon character. Amidst more battles with enemy rockets, the crew receives news that an attempt is imminent at putting a colony on the Moon. Kenmore asserts that a colony there would be safe from enemy attack, but in fact it would be even more vulnerable. There is more tension with the commander, who is picked to lead the first expedition to the Moon.

The pilot of the moon ship makes a mistake and it looks like it will crash rather than land when it reaches its target. Kenmore takes his own ship, a space tug, and catches up to them, planning to use his own engines to compensate for the error and allow the moon ship to land. Brown proves to be a better officer than expected and the two are reconciled.

The novel has most of the same problems as its predecessor – a naïve view of politics, plot elements that could only result from massive intelligence failures, coincidences, and deus ex machina solutions. It is inconceivable that the events in orbit would not hasve triggered a major war on Earth. On the other hand, Sally Holt continues to be a surprisingly intelligent character for a 1950s science fiction female. Although she is off stage most of the time, she contributes several positive ideas and solves at least one major problem.

City on the Moon (1957) was the last in the series. It shares the international paranoia of its predecessors but the plot is somewhat stronger. There are one hundred and fifty men on the moon, drawn from various nations in an attempt to counter the fear caused by the existence of American missile bases hidden among the craters. Someone has been committing sabotage, however, and several moon rovers have gone missing or have been destroyed.

Kenmore and a man named Moreau are returning from a trip when they are nearly killed by a manufactured landslide. They overhear a rocket from Earth desperately trying to communicate with Civilian City, the moon base, but there is no reply and as their damaged rover approaches, the colony looks completely deserted. Kenmore discovers that it was evacuated following sabotage on an even greater scale, although it is never completely clear why they would not have stayed at the base.

The city was evacuated because of air leaks. The rocket landed safely and Sally Holt, Kenmore's love interest, is okay. The evacuees supposedly headed for the missile bases, but they do not arrive and there is concern that they have all died. The small party then struggles to survive under the already unfavorable conditions, exacerbated by more instances of sabotage. They attempt to repair a crashed space shuttle in order to escape back to Earth.

Before they can do so, they encounter a group of scientists who have discovered a process that could literally destroy the universe. The scientists are determined to suppress the discovery and Kenmore believes they have gone mad, committing virtual suicide. The staff at the missile bases have been repairing the sabotage and hope to return the refugees to the city, but they also believe that further experimentation with new energy sources is unwise, which could put an end to the space program. The saboteurs are identified and arrested and at the last moment it is proved that the doomsday prediction was wrong, so research can be resumed.

The Red Scare of the 1950s is clearly evident in the trilogy, which also expresses paranoia about Europeans nations as well. Leinster's handling of international intrigue had not changed much during the decade since *Fight for Life* and *Murder of the USA*, but it would be far less of a story element in the years that followed. This was, however, one of Leinster's less interesting novels despite a fairly good description of the efforts to survive in a hostile environment.

Operation Outer Space (1954) takes place in an overpopulated future in which there is a substantial colony on the moon but limited exploration elsewhere. Jed Cochrane works for an advertising firm who is rather rattled when he is ordered to drop everything and accompany Bill Holden to Lunar City for a mysterious new project. His secretary, Babs Deane, is also on the flight and is far more enthusiastic about it than is Cochrane.

There is a brief stopover at a space station during which Holden explains that the daughter of one of the corporate executives married a man named Dabney, who is reportedly some sort of crackpot. They have been sent to the Moon as part of some as yet unexplained plan to cater to Dabney's ideas for family rather than commercial reasons. It turns out that Dabney actually has made a discovery, a way to communicate faster than the speed of light. Since it only works from vacuum to vacuum, it cannot be used on Earth, but is ideal for outer space.

Dabney's assistant, Jones, insists that it was actually his discovery but he sold the rights to Dabney. He begins to have second thoughts when they discuss the possibly that the same principle could be applied to matter, resulting in faster than light travel. Cochrane decides to form a company and launch the first interstellar expedition and his bosses think it is all just an elaborate plan to soothe Dabney. But the situation changes with a demonstration that proves that the stars are within reach.

Johnny Simms, a rich but amoral man living on the moon to

avoid being arrested, buys a share in the corporation Cochrane founds in order to ensure that he and his wife Alicia are aboard the first flight to the stars. Cochrane, who has quit his job in order to head the new company, is not happy with the prospect. He sells endorsements as the primary source of funding for the operation.

The ship takes off on its maiden flight after Cochrane is lured aboard. Deane has purchased a block of stock so she is there as well. Unfortunately, they lack the capacity to monitor the ship's velocity so they are unable to orient themselves in order to return. Fortunately, they still have instantaneous radio contact with Earth, so an analysis of the star fields should eventually solve the problem by pinpointing their location. They also discover that they are near a fairly Earth type planet.

They land on a world that looks like early Earth, forested and volcanic. They have not brought any equipment with which to test the air, but after some minor investigation they take a chance and find it breathable. Some large creatures resembling bears are spotted but fortunately they decided to bring weapons so they feel safe. Their exploration is uneventful until a major seismic disturbance nearly topples the ship. Jones is forced to take off to avoid a wreck, leaving Cochrane, Deane, Simms, and two others behind.

The ship is able to return and locate them the following day, and in the interim Cochrane has proposed to Deane. They visit a second planet and spot some primitive humanoids. Simms shoots and kills one of them and when Cochrane upbraids him, Simms unilaterally announces that he is taking charge of the expedition. Deane hits him over the head with a chair and he is disarmed.

On the next planet they visit, Simms disobeys orders, goes out to hunt, and is nearly trampled to death in a stampede. He refuses to return to the ship so a search party is mounted. He is found, severely injured, and the experience improves his behavior. A few more planets are briefly surveyed before the ship returns to Earth. All of the partners are now very rich and they give their technological secrets to the world.

Much of the first part of the book is spent describing the process of traveling to the Moon and a surprisingly large amount of it is still scientifically valid. Once again, Leinster uses his female characters sparingly but they are both quietly competent. Cochrane never realizes just how thoroughly Deane is conducting business for him and she has insights that he completely misses.

The Forgotten Planet (1954) is actually assembled from three previously published novelettes. It opens with a prologue in which the unnamed planet is found by a survey ship to be completely lifeless. The process of seeding it is disturbed through an oversight so only insects and fish are introduced. Then a crash landing introduces humans who, after centuries, forget their origin and adapt to the odd ecology.

"The Mad Planet" (1926) is the story of Burl, a young man on that unnamed world (in the original version it is Earth following an ecological catastrophe). He and his tribe lack knowledge of fire, metal, or even stone working, and they have limited vocabularies. Their world consists of giant plants – mostly fungi – and equally giant insects. Burl is wakening to sexual interest in Saya, another member of his tribe, but they have not yet mated.

One day it occurs to Burl that the horn of a dead beetle – which is longer than his arm – could be used as a weapon against some of the less deadly insects. Burl successfully spears a fish but falls into the water and ends up on an improvised raft of fungus drifting toward the unknown. He finally makes it to shore and finds himself in a food rich area. Determined to lead his tribe back here, he starts to follow the river back the way he had come, but is attacked by a three foot long tarantula, which he wounds with his makeshift spear. The two of them fall into the web of an even larger spider, although Burl finally escapes.

Army ants approach and Burl is forced to flee but fire breaks out in the fungus and most of the army is destroyed. Burl kills a spider on his way back to the tribe and by now his thoughts are moving in a way that has not happened in generations. He coerces the other men in his tribe to attack and kill a particularly giant spider that has terrorized them for years and to hunt smaller prey, particularly ants, for food. This constitutes a dramatic societal change.

Burl's adventures continue in "Red Dust" (1927), which opens with an infestation by a new kind of fungus whose spores are poisonous. Burl decides that the tribe must move out of the area, but migration is not a part of their culture and they follow without understanding. One night he unwisely attacks a nocturnal beetle which flies far enough away before crashing that he does not know where he is in relation to the rest of his tribe. But he finds them in time to save an unconscious Saya from some lesser beetles.

The tribe is forced to relocate to escape the spores and after a long trek, they find an area free of them. Burl is somewhat miffed that his leadership is no longer necessary, but the arrival of a giant tarantula alters the situation. Their final adventures constitute "Nightmare Planet." The tarantula has a horde of eggs which hatch, and the tribe must trek again, but this time they leave the fungus forest behind and for the first time emerge into full sunlight. There they find a more Earthlike forest and the descendants of dogs who were with their stranded ancestors and who have survived on their own. They form the expected relationship. The novel ends, rather abruptly and unconvincingly, with a starship landing, finding Burl's tribe, and using technology to educate them so that they can blend into galactic society.

Gateway to Elsewhere (1954) was expanded from the 1951 magazine version published as *Journey to Barkut.* Leinster rarely wrote traditional fantasy and this is his longest, closest effort in that area. Tony Gregg has a lucky piece, a coin marked with Arabic characters, and one day he is told that the translation indicates it was currency in Barkut, although no one has ever heard of Barkut. One day Gregg hears a legend about parallel worlds and is told of a man who might pay a lot of money for his coin because of the possibility that it might provide access to alternate realities.

Gregg has been using flips of the coin to make minor decisions, but now he decides to take it to the race track. There he makes a small fortune in a single day. This convinces him to let the coin decide his fate and not long after we rejoin him somewhere in the Mideast where he has perhaps unwisely taken passage on a ship crewed by cut-throats. He escapes in a small boat, falls asleep, and wakes up in Barkut.

Three men attack him and he is able to kill one and drive the other two away. He takes their camels to the nearby city where he is imprisoned in the belief that he is a djinn and is taught to speak the local language by a slave girl named Ghail. Gregg proves that he is human but is then approached by a female djinn named Nasim.

The king of the djinn has kidnapped the human queen and the leaders of the city want Gregg to lead the fight against them, having accepted his somewhat grandiose stories about his own past. Adding to his problems is the arrival of Es-Souk, a male djinn who was betrothed to Nasim, who has somehow become fascinated with Gregg. They fight but the djinn inexplicably rushes away. Gregg has no idea how he scared the djinn off, but the king of the djinn offers him safe passage for a meeting.

He visits the djinn city and discovers that djinns are atomically unstable and explode catastrophically when they die. Nasim continues to flirt with him. The captive queen admits that she rather likes the djinn and hopes Gregg will not exterminate them. Gregg has secretly brought a substance – ragweed pollen - to which the djinn are violently allergic and he fills his cigarette lighter with the fluid when Es-Souk escapes, although he suspects the djinn king arranged for this to happen to test Gregg's powers.

Gregg defeats and kills Es-Souk and finally is introduced to the king of the djinn. He then uses ragweed to disrupt the court and is proclaimed king of the djinn by all but a few dissidents. These are dealt with when Gregg fools them into destroying themselves. Ghail is revealed to be the rightful queen of Barkut. The woman posing as the queen is actually her aunt, who did so to protect her from the djinn. Gregg and Ghail get married and he figures out how to set up a trading company between the two realities. Light weight and contrived but amusing.

The Planet Explorer (1957, aka *Colonial Survey*) is another fix-up novel consisting of four short stories. "Solar Constant" (1956, aka "Critical Difference") introduced Bordman, who is about to make his first independent planetary survey. He is currently on Lani III, a mostly frozen colony spawned from another planet in the same solar system. The planet is worth the effort to establish a colony because of its mineral resources and Bordman's job is to ensure that the facilities are safe.

The colony receives a message from the home world indicating that sunspots and other changes in the system's star will cause a lengthy period of very intense cold. Most of the population of the original colony world is likely to die and resupply of the smaller colony will become impossible. Bordman points out that the latter would be a good place to test methods of surviving on the larger one before conditions there become critical.

Bordman is in love with a colonist, Riki Herndon, and he plans to force her to leave when the survey ship arrives to pick him up. Spaceships are landed and launched by landing grids, immense structures which tap into the ionosphere for power, but they cannot generate enough to keep the two populations alive in the long run. Bordman finds a way to make vaporous clouds that increase the amount of heat a planet absorbs, which means both worlds can be saved. Landing grids would become a common element in Leinster's science fiction, notably in the Med Ship series.

The story unfortunately contains a mildly misogynistic passage in which Riki contends that women are the first to object to impossible situations but that it is men who deal with them. Bordman marries Riki but is frequently called away for extended duty on other worlds, which sets the stage for the remaining stories.

"Sand Doom" (1955) was actually the first published story in the series and it poses the opposite problem. Xosa is a hot desert planet. Bordman arrives to discover that their landing grid is down and the colony is probably doomed. The ship that brought him is trapped by a special anomaly and cannot leave, nor can a message be sent requesting assistance. An unexpectedly long sandstorm completely buried the landing grid under construction with thousands of tons of sand. The colony has no way to clear the sand away and complete the grid and the abrasive sand is also slowly destroying their other equipment. Bordman and the fifty colonists figure out a way to provide enough cooling to support hydroponics by manipulating how the planet's surface cools during the nights. They also manage to juryrig a landing grid and bring down the ship, which has ample supplies to save them all until other arrangements can be completed.

Although Leinster meant it to be complimentary, his contention that different races have distinctly different talents and abilities is inaccurate. It may have been that he meant that different cultures develop or emphasize different skills, which would make more sense. Xosa was colonized by Native Americans and most other colonies consist of one specific society on Earth so this might well be a factor.

"Combat Team" (1956) won the Hugo Award under its original title, "Exploration Team." A man named Huyghens, an eagle, and a team of mutated bears are the only inhabitants of an illegal "colony" in a remote star system. Bordman is accidentally landed there instead of at a legitimate settlement elsewhere. The authorized colony was heavily dependent upon robots because the planet was considered too dangerous for major human inhabitation and Huyghens speculates that the local predators, sphexes, overwhelmed the compound and possibly killed everyone there.

The two men detect a faint distress signal from the legal colony and decide to mount a rescue operation. Their journey involves some minor adventures and despite Bordman's intention to arrest his companion, they become almost friendly. Together they discover that the sphexes have a vulnerability – they breed in selective places – which provides a means to control or even eradicate them and make the planet safe for a normal human rather than robotic colony. They rescue the survivors and Bordman invents a story that makes Huyghens's presence retroactively legal.

The final story is "The Swamp Was Upside Down" (1956). Bordman is called to the planet which hosts Sector Headquarters for the Colonial Survey, but his landing is delayed while another senior officer is brought down. The planet is mostly water and the small land area where humans have settled is now in danger because the interface between mud and deeper rock has become slippery. Any vibration or loud noise is likely to cause slippage and destruction. There has also been an accident in the fuel storage area which could potentially cause a major explosion. The only obvious solution is to evacuate everyone to the solid land at the poles of the planet. They solve both problems by using the explosive power of the fuel to dry out the slipping soil,

War With the Gizmos (1958, aka *The Strange Invasion*) opens with accounts of the deaths of various wild animals after battles with invisible creatures the author calls Gizmos. Initially no humans are among the dead. Although we are assured in the introduction that the Gizmos were ultimately defeated, we are also told that their origin remains a mystery since it seems unlikely they could have operated a spaceship, or that they could have been living on Earth for long without having been discovered.

Dick Lane is in a rural part of Virginia investigating mysterious deaths of animals and a few humans when he becomes the first person to survive an attack by Gizmos. None of the victims show signs of any wounds but Lane discovers why when an invisible something covers his face, preventing him from breathing. He only escapes because he falls to the ground, his face buried in fallen leaves, and the attacker is thwarted.

He manages to leave the area with a bunch of leaves pressed to his face and finds Professor Ann Warren and her niece Carol. Warren is conducting a biological study in the area. She has already been puzzled by the strange deaths of animals in the wild and rather too easily accepts Lane's story about his experience. They are still talking when a dog is attacked right in front of them and they all take shelter inside Warren's trailer.

Lane notes that a faint whining sound can be heard when the Gizmos attack and Warren points out that they are not completely invisible, that they cause a very slight wavering of light and are probably gaseous. One of them gets inside the trailer and they capture and kill it by wrapping it in a sheet and constricting it until it collapses. They also discover that the Gizmos die if touched by a flame.

Lane suspects that they are more intelligent than mere animals and figures out that they work cooperatively as well as individually. The three humans are trapped inside the trailer as more Gizmos swarm to the area. Over the radio they hear reports of mysterious deaths and radar sightings, but nothing indicating that the public at large knows the nature of the threat. The Gizmos manage a mass break-in, and they replace all the air so that covering one's face is ineffective. Lane passes out and when he wakes, all three of them are prisoners of the Gizmos, who seem to be studying them.

They escape by fashioning torches although the Gizmos follow them constantly. They travel through the night and reach a gas station the following morning. A large number of Gizmos form into one dynamic system and create a dust cloud, but Lane starts a serious fire with spilled gasoline which kills many of them and disrupts their cooperative effort. When the attack is over, the professor uses the telephone to try to spread the alarm, but no one will believe her. The authorities assume that a nationwide increase in unexplained deaths results from some new disease. They leave in a car owned by a stranger named Burke, who has no doubt about the existence of the creatures because of his own recent experiences.

They are pursued by four giant dust clouds produced by the Gizmos but they manage to elude them while arguing about whether they are smart animals or actually intelligent. When they reach a good sized town, they buy torches and other weapons just before the community is attacked by a mass of Gizmos. They kill many of them before they are able to get away in the car but they have also taken one of them captive in a pillowcase.

The number of incidents continues to rise but Lane is primarily concerned with a massive group of Gizmos gathering in a mountainous area. The Gizmos begin targeting vehicles causing accidents and traffic jams across the country, but the true nature of the menace is still unknown except to our heroes. Warren captures another Gizmo but Burke panics and kills it. They do, however, discover that the Gizmos are repelled by garlic.

A major concentration of Gizmos descends upon Chicago and kills everything in the stockyards. This time there accretion was big enough to show up on radar, although its true nature is still a mystery to the authorities. Eventually Lane and the others reach someone who can spread the truth and we are left to presume that the Gizmos were wiped out, although the end is quite perfunctory.

The Pirates of Zan (1959, aka *The Pirates of Ersatz*) is the story of Bron Hoddan, who stows away to escape his homeland on the planet Zan, whose populace is renowned as pirates. He travels to the planet Holden where he hopes to use his considerable engineering talents to make a name for himself in more conventional ways. He settles down and begins to work toward his goal.

Then one morning the police arrest him. They are accompanied by his friend Derec, who explains that Hoddan has inadvertently killed someone and might have been responsible for many more deaths without realizing it. The police are clearly terrified as they search his quarters. There is a hasty hearing at which Hoddan admits that he sabotaged some equipment at the local power company and replaced it with his own, far more efficient invention. The power company had refused to even listen to his presentation. But a dead man has been found near the device and it is believed that it created some sort of death ray. This is such a terrifying prospect that the invention and all records of it have been destroyed. Hoddan is to be imprisoned for life under a technicality so that he can never duplicate his work.

Hoddan escapes and takes refuge as a political dissident at the Interstellar Embassy. He is advised that the nearby planet Darth, which has a feudal society, is looking for an engineer with his qualifications. That night, however, he receives what appears to be a note from Nedda, the woman he loves. It turns out to be a police trap to lure him outside the embassy, but he anticipates that possibility and returns safely after avoiding the men sent to apprehend him.

Another ruse gets him to the spaceport and he is soon on the planet Darth, where he uses stun pistols to thwart an attempt to steal his luggage. He then sets out to find a local aristocrat, Don Loris, who has need of an engineer, assisted by Thal, who is in Loris's service. Thal explains that Loris is feuding with Lord Ghek because the former's daughter, Fani, refuses to marry him.

Loris is upset that stun pistols were used because he fears that word will get out that he has imported weaponry to gain a military and political advantage. He threatens to throw Thal and Hoddan into a dungeon but instead allows them to serve as guards for Fani, who is menaced by kidnappers. Hoddan is also concerned because he saw a group of three spaceships in the sky and suspects they are from Holden and are looking for him.

Raiders kidnap Fani during the night and Hoddan is unable to interfere because he has been locked in his room. Once free, he organizes a pursuit on horseback while Loris seems stunned and ineffectual. They foil an ambush but are unable to stop Ghek from taking Fani into his castle. Hoddan arranges a ruse to get inside and they rescue Fani, loot the castle, and embarrass Ghek.

Unfortunately Hoddan's troubles multiply. Although he sabotages the spaceport control room, a delegation from Walden lands offering a large fee for his capture. Nine other spaceships begin to orbit the planet and it is possible that this is a fleet of pirate ships. But when Hoddan sneaks aboard the landing craft and lifts into orbit, he sees hundreds of ships, most of them elderly, obsolete models.

Hoddan contacts the leaders of the fleet. It is a major planetary population which had planned to relocate to a new world only to discover that the equipment they bought for that purpose is unserviceable and mostly beyond repair. Hoddan convinces them that if they loan him a small space yacht, he will travel to Holden and convince the government there to donate new equipment. He then kidnaps Thal and six other men from Darth and tells them that they have all become space pirates.

Hoddan finds a new way to capture a space liner, then sells its cargo to buy replacement equipment for the traveling fleet, as well as bonuses for his small crew. He returns to Darth to come to an agreement with Loris, but is double-crossed and nearly captured.

Fani helps him to escape by pretending to be his prisoner. But he unwisely rejects Fani in favor of Nedda, who is still on Holden, so when he returns she tries to have him ambushed and killed.

With a fresh crew of impressed pirates, Hoddan follows the ragtag fleet and raids each planet it passes, having spread the rumor that the entire fleet is piratical in order to discourage resistance. They also kidnap Nedda, but Hoddan discovers that they really are not in love. He takes her to Darth and makes peace with Loris and Fani, eventually marrying the latter. His investments have made him so rich that he pays back everyone from whom he stole.

Leinster advances a theme not uncommon in science fiction that the achievement of a high civilization would take most of the interest out of life because there would be few things that were not predictable. Government's primary purpose is therefore to ensure that the status quo is not threatened, even by what might be considered an improvement. The result is that most activity is designed to relieve boredom rather than actually discover anything new. "Taxes are, in part, the insurance premiums one pays for protection against the unpredictable." The novel is an engaging adventure story with touches of humor, but it does rely a great deal on coincidence and luck.

Four from Planet 5 (1959, aka *Long Ago, Far Away*) is a first contact story. The protagonist is Soames, who is in love with Gail Haynes but is too poor to consider marrying her. He works at a meteor tracking station in Antarctica where she is visiting temporarily as part of a public relations program. They are together when an odd signal triggers his equipment, and then loud static emerges from all the speakers – and they will later discover this was true of every radio in the world.

An airborne object appears out of nowhere, slows to a stop, changes directions, and then crashes or at least hits the ground approximately eighty miles from the base. The following day Soames, Haynes, and Captain Estelle Moggs take a helicopter to the site and find a crashed vehicle of unknown design, presumably a spaceship. Four children emerge, so they land, but the children do not understand English. They appear to be alone and the doors and furniture of the ship were clearly not designed for adults. The area immediately surrounding the ship remains warm and calm despite blowing snow all around, apparently protected by some kind of force field.

The children begin erecting what Soames believes is a signaling device. He destroys it, convinced that it would be a disaster if a superior culture were to take an interest in Earth, even benevolently. The children are horrified by his action. They take a few items out of the ship and then use an unknown device to complete destroy the wreckage. They are then evacuated to the American base.

Word of the children's existence leaks to the newspapers, who publish stories warning of invasion fleets and the futility of resistance. The military orders a complete news embargo – Leinster gets this wrong as it would have to be civilian authorities to enforce such a policy. The embargo is a waste of time because the news is already out and the children are barely evacuated to a plane before a Russian assault team arrives under a subterfuge, intending to take them prisoner.

Soames and Haynes suspect the children have some kind of telepathy, because they all know things that only one has been taught. But they talk incessantly nevertheless and they did not know that Soames was planning to destroy their emergency beacon, so it is not clear how this ability functions.

The children are horrified by their first sight of the moon and from this Soames concludes that they are from the past when there was a planet where the asteroid belt is at present. Presumably their civilization knew that it was doomed and was preparing to invade and colonize a future Earth. The signaling device may have been to tell them it was okay to follow, so Soames concludes that they must be prevented from building another. Their secret must not reach the public or they would likely be executed. But he is not sure if they lived on the fifth planet, or if they are part of an older human culture on Earth that was trying to escape the bombardment.

Elsewhere, the Russians are protesting the seclusion of the children and the international situation has grown tense. The decision is made to televise an interview with the children in an attempt to ease tensions. Despite its intention to calm fears, the broadcast exacerbates them and there are riots and other forms of violence. The sequence in which a bunch of rowdy protestors are able to seize some items from the children is forced and not entirely believable.

The revelation that the belts worn by the children can produce a kind of telepathy is revealed on television – no one had realized it before - and this causes even further unrest even though this proves that they cannot actually read thoughts from other people, although they can detect emotions. They are returned to a high security area, but one of the boys – Fran – manages to escape. The children have somehow secretly built communication devices and are in touch with Fran, and they have also given the devices to Soames and Haynes.

Soames is worried that Fran might still be trying to communicate with the past. Soames uses the communicators and common sense to figure out when Fran is. The boy has in fact built a communication device, but it malfunctions. Its operation attracts the authorities but Soames manages to spirit him away.

International politics heat up again because it is now suspected that the children are a hoax and that the US government is working with the real aliens, whom no one else has seen. Soames suddenly figures out that the children are not from a large civilization but part of a relatively small group of about two thousand who managed to survive the initial cataclysm when fragments of the fifth planet began to strike the Earth. So he helps Fran build another communicator to bring the rest of them to the present, and somehow this brings the world crisis to an end, although the details of this transition are not provided.

Within its premise, the novel is quite successful, but some of the plot elements are less than convincing. Soames and Haynes would almost certainly not have been allowed to remain as primary contacts for the children. The government would never have been as lax about protecting them, nor would it have allowed them to retain the mechanical devices whose purpose they did not understand. The ease with which Soames and others find ways to replicate part of the technology is not credible, nor is it likely that the children would have the knowledge to build communication devices from scratch using what to them would be alien technology. Nor would the people in charge of them have missed their existence. The solution is not particularly rewarding, and it seems to have taken the children a long time to learn enough English to explain their situation. And finally, how could humans have already existed at the time the fifth planet exploded?

The Monster from Earth's End (1959) was filmed, quite badly, as *The Navy vs the Night Monsters*. Gow Island is a remote base near the Antarctic, with a complement of fifteen men and four women, including Drake, the commander, and Spaulding, the supply officer, the latter of whom is overdue for leave. Beecham is a scientist studying the island's biology and Nora Hall, the latest to arrive, is a clerk. Spaulding and Drake are both romantically interested in Hall. A plane is due carrying several men scheduled to return to the United States after a long tour in Antarctica, plus specimens of plant life recently discovered in a small region heated by hot lakes.

There is sudden shouting and the sound of gunshots through the radio, then silence. The plane changes course and although it heads toward the island periodically, it always swerves away. Eventually it does crash land on the island, but the pilot promptly shoots himself without offering any explanation. No one else is aboard. One of the five penguins is missing and one bale of the strange trees has been broken open. The door was open before the crash. The wreckage makes it impossible for any other plane to land until it is cleared away so the island is completely isolated until it can be moved or a ship can be sent from elsewhere.

Spaulding's theory is that something flew into the plane and took the men away, the same something that is responsible for other recently missing aircraft, although this is a red herring. The pilot's body is stored in a small warehouse, but the man guarding it panics when he hears something moving nearby. Drake also hears sounds of movement from inside the building, but when he turns on the lights and steps inside, there is no sign of an intruder. The body of the pilot has somehow disappeared.

Drake orders the radar station to be manned constantly. It is sensitive enough to pick up swarms of birds so he is confident it will provide warning if anything approaches. He also has floodlights installed all around the buildings so that nothing can sneak up on them. Guards patrol the perimeter all night but nothing else happens.

In the morning, Drake organizes a search of the island, particularly an area of hot springs and the nesting area for a large colony of sea birds. The authorities are skeptical of the account Drake provided by radio and sends another airplane to the island, but it is unable to land. Although none of the humans notices, one of the dogs encounters a small plant, only inches long, that moves away and hides in a hole in the ground. Beecham arranges to have some of the Antarctic trees temporarily planted at the hot springs so that they can survive.

During the second evening, one of their dogs suddenly begins to scream and disappears before they can find out what is happening. Spaulding has made Molotov cocktails and he uses some of them to illuminate the entire area, but once again nothing appears to be out of place. Despite a thorough search, there is no sign of the attacker or the presumably dead dog.

Although some of the men saw branches thrashing in the forest, none of them saw the agency of that movement. Spaulding theorizes that the creature is invisible. Drake is unconvinced, but then becomes distracted when radar reports that the birds are all flying above their nests, which never happens at night. Later one of the guards disappears and a dog is attacked. Spaulding throws a Molotov cocktail too far and it starts a fire that destroys the radio and the generator, throwing the entire base into complete darkness. Beecham sees what appears to be a small animal of some sort disappear into a hole in the ground.

The next day Spaulding leads a party to the nesting grounds while Drake arranges for makeshift oil lamps in anticipation of the night. They find broken eggs and nests and some dead birds. Beecham spots and digs up one of the smaller creatures, which looks like an animal mimicking a plant. Progress is made moving the crash off the runway, but its radio is also out of commission and can only receive, so it does pick up a message that a destroyer is en route, but several days away.

Two of the smaller creatures are discovered inside the buildings and one outside. When one of the staff members picks one up barehanded, the toxic shock is enough to render him briefly unconscious. Beecham discovers that fuel oil is lethal to the creatures and concludes that they can use that fact to create an impenetrable barrier. Drake leads an expedition to the beach to put up a warning sign for any landing party from the destroyer. Unfortunately, he allows one of the men to butcher a seal for its meat and stay behind the rest of the party.

The lone man does not return. His scream and a gunshot result in the formation of a rescue party but there is no sign of his body. A thicket of trees is disturbed and the men use gasoline to burn it down. Something struggles frantically among the trees, but they cannot identify what it was and only ashes remain when the fire is out. The invisibility theory is considered again.

The plane is finally successfully moved off the runway but a major storm is brewing so no aircraft will be flying. At Beecham's suggestion, pieces of raw meat are placed in various places in a ring of a chemical which is fatal to the small creatures. Dozens of them are found dead within a few hours. Beecham also draws attention to the branches of the last bundle of trees, still firmly tied, the ends of which appear to have broken off. The reader is likely to be well ahead of the characters in guessing that this is the origin of the smaller creatures.

Beecham insists on a brief expedition to the hot springs to examine the replanted trees. When they arrive, the trees are all gone. Beecham and Drake both realize that the trees themselves are the killers, and that they can move. At the nesting area they encounter one of the trees and Beecham is nearly killed before they destroy it. He does suffer a sprained ankle, which means they cannot make it back to the base before darkness.

They manage to get back successfully despite the delay, using gasoline bombs to burn some of the trees. When the storm ends, a plane lands but since Spaulding incinerated all of the dead creatures, there is nothing to prove what happened and the newcomers are skeptical. They take the remaining bale of trees into the plane, along with Drake and Hall. The trees break free in the darkened interior but Hall uses a flare to freeze them while Drake pushes them out to fall into the ocean. The plane returns to the island where the pilot, rather unbelievably, attempts to kill himself. But now, presumably, the authorities will accept the truth. Other than the silliness about men driven to suicide by the sight of ambulatory trees – Drake, Beacham, and the others certainly were not – this is a suspenseful and well constructed novel.

The movie preserves most of the plot, although not always as plausibly as in the book. The story opens as a comedy, with repartee among the crew of the aircraft and the staff on Gow Island. Spaulding is a civilian meteorologist whose interaction with the sexy Mamie Van Doren is painfully badly done. The special effects are so minimal they hardly even register. The idea that the sight of animated plants would drive someone insane is not credible in either the book or the movie, unfortunately. There is a subplot in which the pilot is so shocked that he becomes a homicidal maniac and it is completely absurd. The potential of the novel was completely wasted, not unusual in Hollywood.

Men into Space (1960) was a tie-in to the short lived television program of the same name which dealt with the early stages of the exploration of space. At the beginning, space travel has been limited to robots, but First Lieutenant Ed McCauley is about to be launched on the first manned flight, although the public has not been told about the attempt and will not unless everything goes well. The flight is successful and unremarkable, but it is the first time a man has been in space, an event now obviously outpaced by history.

In the second section, McCauley is now a major. He arrives at his new assignment and discovers that a scheduled rocket launch has been moved up to the following day. Rather unrealistically by today's standards, McCauley – the pilot – has not been informed of this change until he arrives. It is to be the first launch of a rocket that is actually controlled by its pilot, in effect the first real spaceship. McCauley is concerned that not all proper tests will have been completed on time, but a rival nation is planning a launch so the rescheduling was done for political purposes. His co-pilot is Major Furness, a not very competent officer, who is injured when he boards the ship but declines to say anything about it until they are in orbit. Despite fuel problems, McCauley deals with the injured man and finds a way to land safely.

Part three takes place during the construction of a space station. McCauley is in charge and has to deal with parts that are not manufactured correctly and people who do not always obey the safety rules. He and a second man are cast adrift but manage to improvise a way to return to the structure.

McCauley is a colonel serving at the moon colony in part four. He discovers that two of his men – who cordially hate each other – have been sent out together on an otherwise routine mission. He also discovers that their emergency air tanks have fallen off their vehicle and that they will be unable to return to the base. McCauley believes that one of the men deliberately discarded the tanks as an excuse to kill the other, since there will be only enough air for one man. Ultimately the two men cooperate and are rescued.

In the fifth section, McCauley is assigned to the first Venus mission because the scientist in charge, Bramwell, is very difficult to work with and McCauley is thought to have the right personality to deal with him. When Bramwell balks at the last minute, he is effectively shanghaied into space. The idea that any one person would be irreplaceable is, of course, not credible. Despite some difficulties with the ship, they do reach Venus, although they do not land.

The final section is about the first expedition to Mars. A series of petty thefts alarms the crew. McCauley figures out who is responsible and forces him to anonymously return the stolen items, but the man is terrified, steals a landing pod, and is the first man to actually land on Mars, although he dies when his oxygen runs out. None of the events chronicled in the book are taken from scripts used in the television series, although they sometimes run parallel. The show itself was surprisingly dull despite what was at the time unexplored dramatic territory.

The Wailing Asteroid (1960) was filmed, horribly, as *The Terrornauts*. Various stations on Earth pick up a signal that originates in the asteroid belt and which is obviously the product of intelligence. Joe Burke, unaware of this, is romancing his secretary, Sandy Lund, although he is ambivalent about the relationship because of visions he occasionally experiences of an alien landscape. When Burke hears a recording of the signals, he recognizes them as sounds he heard during one of his visions. These unsettled experienced started after his uncle gave him a black cube found in an ancient cave, which was subsequently broken.

Burke begins experimenting with creating devices like those in his dreams, while astronomers pinpoint the exact asteroid from which the signal is being transmitted. A signal is beamed back, which changes the initial transmission to another, equally indecipherable. Burke's newly built device appears to generate enormous amounts of power, but he is secretive about its purpose. He begins to order various pieces of equipment and construction materials and it is soon obvious that he is building some kind of spaceship.

The Russians launch a series of fuel ships followed by a manned probe. Burke tests his new form of propulsion and it works. The signals from space are increasingly menacing – the author does not explain how a series of beeps could be modified to add a threatening tone. The government becomes aware of Burke's project and despite some camouflage, suspects its true nature. They descend upon the project, forcing Burke to take off with Lund, her sister Pam, and two other men, Holmes and Keller, still aboard.

Although the military attempts to shoot them down with missiles, they escape Earth's orbit. Burke contacts the authorities by radio and tells them where to find the plans to build more spaceships, and before long the government claims that his ship was part of a secret American space program. It takes almost two weeks for them to reach the asteroid, an interval which the author wisely passes by quickly.

When they arrive they spot a radio mast and the entrance to an enormous tunnel. Their ship enters the tunnel, which becomes suddenly illuminated and filled with breathable air. Artificial gravity replicates that of Earth. The interior contains numerous rooms, some of them filled with countless mysterious metal spheres. Although deserted, it is obviously a fortress of some sort. The Russian cosmonaut is lost in space and is no longer a factor.

Burke figures out that some sort of hostile fleet is headed toward the fortress. He finds a room full of cubes that resemble the one he broke as a child. They are educational devices and from them he learns how to operate the fortress and discovers that its original garrison moved to Earth and for some reason forgot their own origin. Burke finds a cube that speculates about future weapons the enemy might develop, including one that gives ships the apparent mass of a star so that it can destroy any system it enters. The equipment plotting the enemy fleet suggests that they have developed this level of technology and are preparing to annihilate the entire solar system.

The humans begin transmitting data to Earth, but there is not much time before the enemy fleet will arrive. Lund runs into a large, living bird inside the station but it flees. Pam disappears and a short time later Lund is missing as well. They also find a matter transmitter that takes them to one of the planets of the lost civilization. They return to the station and find a way to use the mysterious globes to turn the power of the enemy ships back on its origin and they are all destroyed.

Leinster seems to have become a bit cynical in this one. He describes the world as increasingly selfish. The established nations are no longer interested in spreading freedom and fewer people are willing to actually do something to preserve civilization. Scientists and politicians are more interested in preserving their position in society than in discovering the truth. The public reaction to the news of the signals quickly turns anti-science and violently so. There is also some patronizing comments about women. One of the reasons the garrison fell apart was because women were introduced to the installation.

The 1967 movie version – terrible despite the screenplay by John Brunner - was titled *The Terrornauts*. The tag line was "The virgin sacrifice to the gods of a ghastly galaxy." Not much of the original plot survives – and only Burke and Lund even appear. Burke is a scientist at an observatory and Lund is a secretary. He did have dreams of an alien world, but he does not build a spaceship based on knowledge derived from those dreams.

Instead of traveling on their own, our heroes are kidnapped by a spaceship crewed by robots that look a lot like Daleks from the Doctor Who series. The effects are so bad that in one scene smoke from an explosion goes BEHIND the moon in the sky above. There is also a comic relief auditor whose presence just cheapens an already ridiculous effort. The spaceship actually looks more like a teapot than a saucer. They have to solve a series of puzzles, one of which involves the absolutely worst looking alien creature of all time. One of the tests involves an hallucination, but the hallucination manipulates something solid, which clearly argues that it had to have been real and material.

Lund falls onto a matter transmitter and finds herself on the planet Burke dreamed about. He follows but she has been captured by primitive humanoid natives, from whom he rescues her. In contrast to the book, the fortress was not built by humans. A memory cube explains how to fight the enemy fleet. A remarkably silly looking space battle ensues but all of the enemy ships, along with the fortress, are destroyed.

Creatures of the Abyss (1961, aka *The Listeners*) is the story of Terry Holt, who sells electronic devices in the Philippines and who was recently involved in some kind of controversial activity, although the police accept that he was not technically breaking the law. He is in the process of closing down the store that he ran until his partners attracted police attention. Then a young woman enters, looking for someone who can manufacture a custom electronic device for her father's schooner. It is to be a sonic transmitter that will effectively drive fish in a specified direction. Holt jokingly mentions that the ellos, might not like it, the ellos being the subject of a local superstition about intelligent creatures living in the ocean.

Holt explains that one of the local fishing boats has found a place or a method that results in bulging holds full of fish on every voyage. The other fishermen have tried to follow the lucky one, but they have radar and elude their pursuers in the darkness. When the other fishermen tried to buy radar, the crew of the first objected and this resulted in several fights and arrests. Holt's partner took all the money and absconded, and Holt has decided to shut down temporarily until the conflict is resolved.

Although Holt suspects the woman knows more than she is revealing, he agrees to build the device. The local police chief drops in a short time later and is clearly encouraging him to do so, although he refuses to explain his enthusiasm. When Holt boards the ship, he is greeted by a man named Davis, the woman's father, and told that they can get any equipment he desires and that they have already arranged for his luggage to be brought aboard. Holt rebels and threatens to leave, but when they make it clear that they will not stop him and that they have good reasons for not telling him the whole story, he agrees to remain aboard – although he warns them he will try to figure everything out.

The woman, Deirdre, acquired the equipment from a US Navy ship because her father's mission is of interest to the government and he has some influence with the Navy. Davis suggests to Holt that this might have something to do with the legend of the ellos, but he does not explain further. Holt sets to work making the underwater broadcaster and learns that they are headed for the area where the very lucky fishing boat gathers its catch, which sometimes includes very unusual fish.

Holt finds cryptic references to foam appearing in open sea, the disappearance of a ship that apparently vanished abruptly into the water rather than sinking, and sees photographs of some strange spherical object. The yacht reaches an area where fish are gathered in unbelievable numbers, circling in apparent panic, and when the humans touch the water, they feel a painful prickling sensation.

The circle of fish begins to contract. A humming sound can be discerned, and occasionally a kind of mooing. Davis tells Holt that the sphere in the picture is one of several found attached to fish. They have incredible interior pressure and efforts to open them have resulted in small explosions and their complete destruction. Some sort of giant object erupts from the water briefly, then falls back, and all of the captured fish are sucked down into the depths. Deirdre later tells him that more meteorites fall near the Luzon Deep than anywhere else on Earth.

They stop at an island where a scientific station has found deep sea fish in a shallow cove. A meteorite lands in the ocean that night and its track suggests that it slowed down during entry. Holt discovers that the strange sound/tingling phenomenon is holding fish captive in the cove. He uses his new device to herd the fish in the lagoon into one small section and the others catch a number of unusual specimens, some of which have the mysterious spheres attached to them.

Although no one talks openly about their suspicions, it is clear that they all believe that aliens are visiting Earth. The meteorites have been slowing so that they all land in approximately the same place. The spheres record and transmit data and are obviously some sort of spy device. The deep sea fish were trapped in the lagoon near the station so that surface activity could be monitored.

Another ship arrives and lowers a bathyscape, which is virtually destroyed by an unknown attacker that appears to have bitten through its reinforced shell. Fortunately no one was aboard. Another meteorite is spotted and Holt makes a public prediction that it will land at specific coordinates, using his friend the police chief to make sure that his prediction is well known.

Holt and Deirdre go for a swim after the event is over and he is attacked by an unidentified but very large creature with some sort of tentacle. Holt uses his transmitter to drive it to the surface where it is revealed to be a giant squid. He and other men from the ship are able to kill it with explosive shells. A short time later, a number of very large objects begin to rise from the depths. Holt and the others theorize that the aliens are from Jupiter and seek high pressure and darkness.

More and even larger giant squids reach the surface and attack a fishing boat. An aircraft carrier arrives and launches air strikes. A short but intense battle follows and the carrier is almost sucked down into a column of escaping gas. A mine layer begins dropping explosives and since the aliens are sensitive to pressure, they cannot stand concussions. More than two dozen spaceships emerge from the ocean and vanish into the sky. They are tracked headed for both Venus and Jupiter and there were two different types, so it is assumed that two different races were colonizing the ocean.

This was a nicely suspenseful novel, although there are some awkward moments early on. There is absolutely no reason why Holt could not have been told the story from the outset. Even after the sighting of the aliens, the others withhold information. The only purpose this serves is to maintain some mystery for the reader. Internally, it makes no sense within the context of the story. There is another instance of gender stereotyping. Leinster asserts that men do not change their behavior based on the marital status of people they are with, but that women do.

Operation Terror (1962) sets up a situation for its readers, then yanks the rug out from beneath their feet. Lockley is a cartographer mapping the Boulder Lake area while wrestling with doubts about his impending marriage. He has recently met Jill Holmes and cannot get her out of his thoughts even though she also is engaged. Elsewhere a series of radar reports indicate that a large object is arriving from outer space and that it is decelerating, suggesting that it is under power, and that it will probably come to Earth somewhere in Colorado.

The object reportedly lands and a considerable impact is registered, although no one actually witnesses the event except Vale, Holmes' fiancé. Lockley contacts Vale by radio and is told that an object crashed into Boulder Lake and then floated to the surface. Alien creatures have emerged and have begun to build some sort of structure on the shore. Lockley subsequently hears about the radar sightings and reconsiders his initial impression that Vale had lost his mind.

Lockley calls Vale again and hears the sound of a struggle before he is cut off. Orders are issued to evacuate the area, but Lockley decides to go first to the camp where Holmes has been working to make sure she is safe. He passes a large number of vehicles evacuating the area, but Holmes is not among the passengers. One of the drivers tells him that three men went to investigate the explosion and did not return, and two others were found hallucinating, although they recovered.

Lockley presses onward toward the lake, but a reckless driver forces him off the road and he has to walk the rest of the way. The population at large has been told that aliens have landed and that major military movement is underway, and naturally the rumors are even more frightening than the official story, which is changed to say that it was just a meteorite and that it was being investigated.

Holmes is there by herself, having stayed behind so that Vale can rescue her, which is both silly and rather inconsiderate even if Vale had still been around. She mentions that he tried to talk her into leaving the day before, but does not mention why. Lockley describes the abrupt end of his radio communication with Vale and he has Holmes set off for his disabled car while he checks out Vale's camp site.

The campsite shows signs of disturbance including a smashed radio and strange footprints. There is a sudden stench and then flashing lights and sounds that literally paralyze him. When he regains consciousness, he has been bound and blindfolded and is being carried. He is taken to a featureless metal building where the three missing men untie him and recount similar experiences. Vale is not there. None of them actually saw their captors.

The building is just a dome so they tunnel out at night and scatter. Lockley finds a note from Holmes indicating that she saw something inhuman moving near the camp, and hours later he finds her further down the road near his car. There is too much damage to the vehicle, so the two of them begin walking. Holmes has a portable radio and they hear reports that the government has acknowledged that aliens have landed. Lockley considers the alternate possibility – that this is a hoax perpetrated by the Russians.

They take to the woods, intending to walk to safety, and detect a projected beam of bad smells and paralyzing lights interdicting the nearby highway. Lockley builds an SOS sign on some open ground but when a plane arrives, it is driven off with the terror ray. A helicopter is brought down and its crew is captured, one of them allowed to broadcast a radio message in which he mentions that he has been blindfolded and has not seen his captors.

Something moves from the lake to one of the nearby evacuated towns, projecting the terror beam in all directions. When it leaves, there is evidence that some buildings have been searched but there is no damage. They do, however, project their beam further and hundreds of people are temporarily paralyzed. Lockley and Holmes reach a farmhouse and have a meal, but no one is around and the telephone does not work.

They are picked up by a large truck whose driver tells them that he is delivering supplies for the Army. Lockley is suspicious of the driver, particularly when he reacts visibly to the possibility that the invaders are actually human. The truck stops in another deserted town where they find a drunk sleeping it off in one of the buildings. While the two men from the truck are dealing with him, Lockley and Holmes find a working telephone line and reach military headquarters. Lockley explains his observations of the terror beam and recounts his experiences, but is met with hostility when he suggests that he is convinced that humans are working with the invaders.

Holmes discovers that the truck is filled with men and electronic equipment, Lockley knocks out the driver and takes his weapon. They manage to escape after Lockley fires several rounds into the truck to disable what he believes is the terror beam generator. They find a ham radio and broadcast a message, then hot wire a car. They hide in another house with the car in the garage. A radio broadcast indicates that the government has duplicated the terror beam.

Lockley rather unrealistically figures out how to counter the terror beam using common household items. He is testing it when Holmes is grabbed and driven off in a car. He also builds something that makes explosives detonate from a distance and then disables two of the vehicles driven by what he assumes are collaborators. He eventually reaches a military base where Vale, Holmes, and others use a loudspeaker to insist that everything is all right, that the whole invasion was a fake. The terror beam was invented by a foreign power as well as the United States and the entire operation was designed to convince other nations to adopt the appropriate defensive systems. The final bit of fakery is the launching of a rocket that is supposed to be the aliens retreating into outer space. Holmes breaks her engagement to Vale in Lockley's favor.

Although fairly suspenseful as it proceeds, the revelations at the end are disappointing and mostly absurd. Lockley's assumption that humans are involved is plucked out of the air and has no rational basis, even though he is mostly correct. The premise that the government would use such a dangerous, roundabout, and implausible method of achieving what could have been done by a simple demonstration of the new weapon is completely unbelievable.

The idea that a secret of this magnitude could be kept is even more so.

Talents, Incorporated (1962) starts with an interplanetary war. Kandar is a relatively peaceful planet on the verge of surrendering to the Mekinese, ruled by a dictator who has already subjugated nearly two dozen worlds. Captain Bors is anticipating the occupation of his homeland by destroying confidential papers that might endanger spies working inside the Mekinese empire when a space yacht arrives carrying a man named Morgan. Morgan is the head of Talents, Incorporated. He is accompanied by his daughter Gwenlyn.

Morgan gives Bors information about Mekinese spies and ship movements in order to establish the accuracy of his intelligence. He reveals the existence of an enemy ship already on the planet, which results in its destruction. The government of Kandar is split about whether or not to resist, but the military has already vowed to fight to the death. Morgan tells Bors that his organization might be of further help to them. He employs people who have unusual psi talents, like dowsing, the ability to predict the arrival times of spaceship, and other oddities.

Morgan provides a mathematical whiz who calculates a new and more effective method of firing missiles in space, which gives the small Kandar fleet a chance of inflicting considerable damage on the attackers. In fact they are able to annihilate the fleet sent against them, but their leaders are not sure if this was a good idea, since Mekin will now want to avenge their losses and prevent other subject planets from thinking there is hope of liberation.

The plan is to conceal the fact that their fleet survived. Bors is to take his ship and pretend to be the sole survivor turned pirate, so that he can capture supply ships and provide food to support the hidden fleet. Their first such effort is a complete success. He captures a supply ship, unsettles a repressive planetary government, and ambushes a warship. One of the talents is aboard and discovers a way to reconfigure their space drive to make it more efficient.

They visit a second subject planet and capture another supply ship, but their plan to escape an enemy battleship goes awry. Although they destroy their opponent, there is a technical problem on their own ship. With their space drive ruined, the remaining crew transfers to the ship commanded by Gwenlyn and their own ship is blown up to prevent salvage by the Mekinese.

The government of Kandar, however, has decided that the fleet should go into exile to prevent Mekin from exacting vengeance against the civilian population. Morgan suggests that this decision might be changed, thanks to his precognitive ability and the efforts of another psi talent, a woman who can project her daydreams onto other people. Bors is uncomfortable about precognition because it suggests that free will is an illusion.

With a new ship, Bors attacks a Mekinese squadron and destroys it using the newly devised tactics. All but one ship are destroyed, but that one escapes into overdrive and is capable of reporting the new tactical advantage. Bors travels to Mekin's home system and captures several cargo ships before leaving, their presence having gone undetected.

They arrive at a new subject planet and discover that it has just overthrown its rulers. The populace knows about Bors' adventures and that the Kandaran fleet was not destroyed. The contagious daydreamer has been at work, but this convinces the government of Kandar that it must immediately surrender. Morgan is troubled because two precognitives have apparently contradictory visions of the future.

A plan is concocted to surrender the fleet in return for assurances about the safety of the civilian population. This is not credible based on the previous events in the book, which make it quite clear that the Mekinese do not feel bound by any agreements they have made. In fact they do attack with a squadron which is virtually wiped out. A holdout ship from another planet arrives at Kandar and pledges to follows Bors' orders.

Kandar launches a fleet of drones when the Mekinese main fleet arrives. The latter destroy all the unmanned ships, pledging to spare the planet, but of course they renege immediately, believing that there is no one left to oppose them. The real fleet attacks and, thanks to the advances provided by the talents, the Mekinese are virtually wiped out. Bors and Gwenlyn end up rather perfunctorily as a couple.

Although this is a minor novel –and the presence of the talents makes the end a foregone conclusion – it is not without some intermittent charm and in some ways resembles the author's Med Service series. Bors is a bit of a chauvinist – he resents having to accept assistance from a woman – though not a misogynist.

The Duplicators (1964, aka *Lord of the Uffts*) is a short, humorous space adventure. After a drunken riot, Link Denham discovers that he has signed on as astrogator and sole crewmember of a broken down spaceship commanded by a man named Thistlethwaite. They are en route to Sord, an uncharted planet known to have been colonized, but also known to be hostile to visitors. Thistlethwaite insists that the planet is the source of an incredibly valuable cargo which he does not immediately identify.

After a tedious and uncomfortable trip, they arrive at Sord and are able to land near a village. Thistlethwaite goes off to make contact and Denham has a brief, enigmatic conversation with two individuals who vaguely resemble pigs and who mentions the uffts. Then a human delegation arrives, without Thistlethwaite but with his weapon and some of his clothing. Denham is understandably wary.

The delegation is headed by Harl and it is soon evident that the planet has a complex code of ethics and that Thistlethwaite violated it by offering to pay for services. Payments are only made to uffts, and while Denham still has no idea what that means, he plays along. He agrees to visit Harl's household, which means a trip through an ufft village. The uffts are the piglike creatures who speak but have no hands and who shout anti-human slogans. Denham uses a riddle to get them preoccupied, but Harl is confused and decides that both he and Thistlethwaite should be hanged.

Denham tries to convince Thistlethwaite to apologize. He also discovers that the local people have matter duplicators. They can make exact copies of whatever they want, so long as they have other items with the same elements. Unfortunately for them they have no way of identifying trace elements, so some things are not as good as their originals, and the originals are gradually fading in quality as they get older. Since there is no incentive to develop or maintain a highly technical civilization, the humans have forgotten how to do so. And commerce is conducted only with the uffts, who have a fondness for beer. If the technology existed elsewhere in the galaxy, it would likely destroy civilization.

Thistlethwaite bribes some of the uffts to allow him to escape. Denham thinks that he plans to take the secret of matter duplication back to sell elsewhere and Denham is determined to stop him even if that means that they are both trapped permanently on Sord. Thistlethwaite makes it back to the ship and rewards the uffts, which makes things even more difficult for Harl. Denham frames Thistlethwaite so that the uffts will believe he is planning to enslave them.

The uffts announce that they are all on strike. Denham manages to organize them into a makeshift revolutionary committee that has them more interested in protocol and speeches than in actually doing anything. Eventually he bargains with Thistlethwaite and takes possession of the spaceship upon which he and Harl's sister leave the planet, after the two sides have returned to equilibrium. The whole story is rather silly but it has its amusing moments and the satire is obvious.

The Other Side of Nowhere (1964, aka *Spaceman*) opens with the protagonist, Braden, hoping to get a berth on the spaceship Rim Star. There are rumors that the ship is going to make a possibly suicidal landing on a distant planet in order to deliver the materials to build a landing grid. Braden is attacked by several men as he approaches the ship, but he is stronger and faster than they are and disables them. One of the attackers realizes that Braden is not even the person they were planning to waylay.

Despite some odd unresolved questions, Braden signs on as mate. On his way back to his quarters, he finds one of the crewmen badly beaten and calls an ambulance. When the ship takes off the following day, the crew is one short and Braden is not confident of the quality of the men. The captain is brusque and seems to rely heavily on the steward. A small number of passengers have also been taken aboard over the captain's objections.

The ship takes off safely. The captain obliquely warns Braden to keep his personal weapon with him at all times, but when Braden goes to his cabin, he discovers that it has already been stolen. He also suspects that the five remaining crew members are the same people who attacked him the day before.

The passengers are a film crew and among them is Derr Carmody, a famous video star. They want to start working during the flight but Braden is skeptical that the captain will allow it. Braden faces down the crew and confiscates a number of weapons, then searches the steward's quarters and retrieves his own. He recommends to the captain that they return for a new crew, but the captain is not pleased with Braden's efficiency. He apparently chose the five unreliable men for a specific reason which he will not explain, and he also orders Braden not to interfere with the steward.

Shortly afterward Braden gives the spare weapons to the passengers and disables the listening device in his cabin. The captain then tells him the truth. His wife and daughter were killed years earlier when a piratical crew took over their ship. He has been tracking them ever since and the five crew members and the steward are almost certainly the pirates. The captain plans to kill them all, even if the ship is lost in the process, and he wants Braden to use the lifeboat to take the passengers to safety if necessary.

Then Braden discovers that the coffee has been drugged and warns the captain. The crew attacks and are initially repulsed by the power weapons held by Braden and the passengers. The captain kills one of the men but is shaken when he finds evidence that the steward may have anticipated his plans. He and Braden are besieged in the control room when the crew makes use of the heavy weapons that the captain thought he had adequately concealed. At least one of the lifeboats has also been sabotaged.

The captain turns over command to Braden and sets out to hunt down the pirates. He intends to harry the pirates while Braden manages to get the passengers to at least temporary safety. The captain has also disabled the second lifeboat which the crew planned to use after they were finished with the ship. He captures one of them and uses him for bait to lure the others into a trap, having also sabotaged most of the ship's internal lights.

The climax comes when the passengers use their special effects equipment to fool the crew into believing they have arrived in the Other Side of Nowhere, a supposed part of space where all the natural laws run backward. The mutineers are overcome in the subsequent confusion and the ship is retaken. The ship successfully reaches its destination and lands and Braden ends up with Derr Carmody's daughter.

There is another instance of patronizing chauvinism typical of the time. "When a man admits that a woman is a better man than he is, he may be honest, but he should be ashamed." Other than that, the story is well plotted and executed, although perhaps a bit padded in a few places with unnecessary detail about the functioning of a spaceship.

Time Tunnel (1964) appeared almost simultaneously with the television show of the same name, which was reportedly inspired by the 1964 movie, *The Time Travelers*. Leinster later wrote two tie-in novels for that series, which only lasted a single season, *The Time Tunnel* and *Timeslip!*. Neither of these is related to this novel.

The protagonist is Harrison, who is in Paris conducting research that has led to some frightening conclusions which are not immediately revealed to the reader. Coincidentally he is mulling the situation over when he runs into an old friend, Pepe Ybarra, whom he knew from his college days. After reminiscing, Harrison explains that he has been investigating old manuscripts and has discovered references to correspondence with various early 19th Century thinkers by a man named Bassompierre, correspondence which describes germs as the cause of disease, explains some of the basics of electricity, and talks about other matters that clearly were far beyond their time.

Harrison expands upon his theme, including advance knowledge that Maximilian would become emperor of Mexico, but just as he says that, he realizes that there never was such a person. The experienced science fiction reader will realize that history just changed. Harrison further theorizes that only time travel would explain what he has found, but Bassompierre was a known historical figure with confirmed dates of birth and death, so it does not seem possible that he could have traveled from the future.

Ybarra knows of a shop which sells antiques and which claims to trade with the year 1804, although both men assume this is an advertising gimmick. They visit the shop and run into Valerie, who works there and is another old friend Harrison had known while living in Paris as a child. Many of the items in the shop are hand made and authentic in appearance but are selling for very small sums. Ybarra is convinced that the shop owners are taking advantage of some ignorant craftsman, but Harrison notices that the "replica" newspapers are printed on antique style paper that is only a few weeks old.

They return to the shop and talk to Valerie, who tells them that her uncle acquires the merchandise but has never told her where it comes from. In due course they discover that the uncle is Henry Carroll, a distinguished professor of methodology. Since they both studied under Carroll, they decide to pay him a visit. He welcomes them both, and when Harrison repeats the string of events involving Bassompierre, Carroll reluctantly admits that he may be responsible, though indirectly.

There is no such thing as a time machine, he explains, but there are places on Earth that can be made to function as tunnels to the past. He has found one of them and his wife's brother has been buying merchandise in the past to sell in the present. He denies, however, any connection to Bassompierre and concludes that someone else has found a bridge to 1804, or perhaps has access to the one he is using. Their situation is complicated by the fact that they have just captured a burglar named Albert who had broken into the hidden tunnel in search of loot, although he does not appear to understand what he has found.

Harrison points out that they can release Albert because he does not know enough to be dangerous and he is in any case a known criminal and is unlikely to be believed. He and the others conclude, however, that Bassompierre must be stopped before he seriously distorts history. This crisis is based on an interpretation of time that assumes ripple effects caused by changes rather than an instantaneous rewriting of history. This is a necessary literary device, but it does not make much sense logically.

Harrison agrees to join Carroll on a journey back through time to find out where Bassompierre is getting his information. Ybarra and Carroll's brother-in-law are both alarmed by the possibility that their ancestors might be injured or killed during one of the visits from the future, cancelling out their existence. Harrison is also concerned that Carroll's wife might sabotage their plans, or even try to kill her own husband to prevent him from carrying them out, because she does not want them to stop bringing trinkets forward so that they can be sold in the shop. There is also by now an emerging theme of the present world hurtling toward self destruction now that the Chinese have exploded a nuclear weapon.

Their assumption that Albert would remain silent proves to be incorrect. A short visit to the past uncovers the clothing that he was wearing when they captured him, which suggests that he returned and disappeared into 1804. Carroll and Harrison visit the past and discover that the local citizenry are actively searching for Albert, whose larcenous habits have caught up to him. They find him first and help him to escape back to the present.

Valerie experiences a time shift in which the shop is changed and she never met Harrison. Time recovers from the change and restores the previous history, and that of Mexico has also righted itself, but Harrison and Carroll are concerned that there are limits to the ability of time to compensate for changes. They prepare for an extended stay in the past to track down Bassompierre. Albert is to accompany them disguised as their servant, a decision which is not really justified by the situation but which is convenient to the plot.

Albert's less savory talents prove useful as they strive to fit in without attracting attention. They are set upon by bandits while on the road, but fortunately brought period pistols with which to drive them off, although they are nervous about killing anyone and changing history. While they are gone – although "while" has an uncertain meaning in this context – the international situation takes a turn for the worst with an apparent missile launch.

Harrison secures an introduction to Bassompierre from an influential Parisian merchant. Nuclear war seems inevitable in the present, however, and Harrison wants to bring Valerie back to the past, while Ybarra and Albert argue that they should try to change history to prevent the crisis from arising in the future. Harrison returns to the present to find that nuclear war is almost certainly imminent.

Albert decides to remain in the present, but Harrison intends to escape into the past. He and Valerie use the tunnel, which collapses behind them. They track down Bassompierre and get involved in a jewel theft before Tallyrand himself shows up and insists that the man is a fraud, that Carroll is actually Bassompierre. The fake Bassompierre draws a weapon and Harrison kills him defending Valerie. A new tunnel is found and all but Carroll return to the present where they learn that the Chinese never developed an atomic bomb and the world is safe. The explanation of the change is rather farfetched and the end is somewhat anticlimactic.

Invaders of Space (1964) is a space opera. Horn is an engineer on Fomalhaut III (this is misspelled Formalhaut throughout the book which is probably the publisher's fault) and is present at the spaceport when an obsolete ship in need of major repairs lands. Horn is anxious because his fiancé's ship is also due in and while space travel is generally safe, accidents do occur. The present ship, the Theban, has an impatient captain who is unreasonable about a projected delay of a few hours before repairs can get underway.

Horn refuses their offer to pay him to patch the engines because only a complete overhaul would make them safe. He thinks that is the end of the matter until he starts home and is promptly shanghaied. When he wakes up the ship is in space and Captain Larsen and the crew pretends that he is a stowaway. Horn beats the captain physically but there is ultimately a standoff. The engines are likely to fail without his help, which would kill them all.

The ship is bound for Hermas, an uninhabited planet that is also host to an automatic beacon so that starships can orient themselves. Larsen offers to cut him in on a large payoff for an unspecified mission, and Horn hints that he is amenable, but he is more concerned because they will arrive at the beacon just before his fiancé's ship is due to pass, and that does not seem likely to be a coincidence. Some of the men aboard inform him readily that they have committed major crimes on a regular basis.

By the time they land on Hermas, the crew recognizes that without Horn they will probably die. He watches silently as the crew destroys the emergency food and fuel stores, and is then stunned when the Danae, carrying his fiancé, radios a distress call. It is automatic, however, as everyone had previously left in lifeboats. One man goes aboard and lands the ship safely. According to the log, the engines failed, although they came on again after everyone was gone. The ship was carrying a large amount of currency, which is Larsen's objective, but the crew took it with them when they evacuated. Clearly Larsen arranged for the false alarm, but did not anticipate that the funds would be removed.

The Theban sets out to find the lifeboats. They are most probably on Carola, another uninhabited beacon world. Horn continues to sow discord among the crew, and he is openly defiant of Larsen and the first mate, because killing him would almost certainly cost all of their lives within hours. The lifeboats are there as expected, but they are empty of both passengers and money. Carola is a jungle planet, so when Horn sets out alone to find his fiancé, he has some minor adventures with the local wildlife.

Horn joins the fugitives and finds that their plans are rather vague. The crew of the Theban disable some of the lifeboats and continue their efforts to find the castaways, but without success. The rainy season has started and the ground is swampy, which makes it difficult to search systematically. Horn arranges for them to find some of the money, just enough that quarrels begin to erupt. He also clandestinely alters the message that the beacon is sending.

One of the Theban crewmen, the engineer Horn replaced, had come with him because he was afraid that Larsen would kill him for his incompetence. But he disappears and Horn realizes that he has decided to try to get back into the captain's good graces by telling him where they are. Although they delay things by moving their camp, all but Horn are eventually captured. Horn is taken as well when he tries to rescue them, but Larsen tries to double-cross his crew and leave them behind on the planet. He is alone with Horn, who is injured, but who manages to use the ship's artificial gravity to incapacitate Larsen. He forces him out onto the planet's surface, then takes the people from the Danae off planet in Larsen's ship. Presumably the crew will kill Larsen before the authorities arrive to arrest them.

The Greks Bring Gifts (1964) is a first contact story. An enormous starship appears near the moon and, after two days of silence, transmits a message indicating that they are a training ship from elsewhere in the galaxy, that they encountered humanity by accident, and that they would like to land and talk in person. The aliens, who call themselves Greks, insist that they are wholly altruistic and have no hostile intentions. The narrator makes it clear, however, that this was not the case but that humanity was fooled for a time.

The Greks provide a great deal of knowledge – broadcast power, cost effect desalinization, new materials and techniques. The Greks remain for six months and while they are themselves somewhat physically repulsive though humanoid, most contact is through the Aldarians aboard their ship, supposedly cadets being trained for space travel. Jim Hackett, a scientist, and Lucy Thale, his girlfriend, decide to participate in the enormous planetwide party when the ship finally announces its departure.

Jim has mixed feelings about the Greks. Their gifts have caused enormous social displacements. Most doctors are out of work and other industries have disappeared entirely. Many scientists have abandoned their research. But everyone likes the Aldarians, although it is not clear why they have ears since they are universally deaf. One Aldarian is driving in heavy traffic and has an accident. Jim and Lucy rescue him and take him to the hospital, where he briefly speaks to Lucy – which is unprecedented – and secretly gives her something before the Greks arrive to take him to their ship.

Jim theorizes that the Aldarian did not want the Greks to find the object – which for some reason Jim does not express any wish to see. He and Lucy join a group of scientists who are planning to examine the trash left behind by the Greks when their ship leaves. The Greks broadcast an appeal for Jim and Lucy to come to the ship to be "thanked" but neither of them is interested.

After the ship leaves, the garbage pit is excavated. It contains the bodies of several Aldarians who have clearly been tortured and executed. There is evidence that the Greks had secretly visited various parts of the planet, and there are there human bodies which have obviously been dissected for study. Later there are more Aldarian bodies including women and children.

Jim discovers that his car has been booby-trapped, apparently by humans working for the Greks. There is a rather extended and not completely convincing account of how the FBI manages to trick the assassins into revealing themselves. An autopsy of the dead Aldarians reveals that their deafness was created surgically.

The rest of the world is unaware of these discoveries and the global economy continues to plummet. Rather implausibly, no one except Lucy appears to remember that the Greks left some Aldarians on Earth and that they have no reason to love their rulers. But the counter argument is that undoubtedly the Greks are holding hostages to keep them from revealing any of their secrets. The device Lucy received from the dead Aldarian does not seem to function, nor is there any hint of its purpose.

Signals are detected which indicate the Greks did not leave and are hiding behind the moon, waiting for human society to collapse so that they can take over. Lucy figures out that the mystery device is a hearing aid designed to circumvent Grek imposed deafness. Jim is rather improbably trained to break into the power station run by the Aldarians to try to figure out their technology. He is amateurish and spotted almost immediately, but the Aldarians pretend not to have seen him.

He discovers that the station is a fake, that the power is being broadcast from elsewhere. All over the world, people begin to reverse engineer Grek technology. Lucy has another breakthrough and Jim realizes that the Greks are not as bright as formerly believed. They made a single lucky discovery that they are using to provide the illusion of an entire new technology.

The real generator of the beamed power is in the Arctic and a secret expedition is sent to capture it. The other secret bases are occupied before they can raise the alarm and one of the Aldarians stationed there agrees to tell them the truth. When the Grek ship returns to "save" Earth from itself, the part of the ship housing the Greks is destroyed by missile fire and the Aldarian slaves are set free. Although this is not a bad story, it requires quite a suspension of disbelief and a blind eye to its inconsistencies, like why the Greks would deafen the Aldarians to prevent them learning things that they learn anyway by seeing them.

Space Captain (1965) is a slight expansion of the serial *Killer Ship*. Captain Trent of the spaceship Yarrow is descended from a long line of successful space captains. His employers want him to conduct a risky trading mission which will also test out a new system designed to discourage space pirates. The region to which he is supposedly going is plagued with them and interplanetary commerce has ground to a halt. Trent is aware of the fact that the owners hope he will disappear so they can claim the insurance, but he is circumspect in his initial landings.

Trent trains his crew to fight inside a spaceship and defend it from pirates, but they are convinced that he plans some piracy of his own. A short time later they stumble upon a pirate ship looting a disabled merchant vessel. The new device shorts out immediately so Trent rams the enemy ship, which escapes into hyperspace, then offers to take the survivors of the other ship aboard. He moves the derelict so that the pirates cannot return and loot it.

The rescued people include the daughter of the president of Loren, a world which has been so isolated that it hired a privateer to steal supplies. The pirate that attacked them pretended to be the very same privateer – and it is possible that it actually was. After dropping off the rescued people, Trent tracks down the now derelict ship and boards it with a small prize crew to repair the engines and bring it to some planet as salvage. He leaves his own ship under the command of his first mate with instructions for a rendezvous.

The repairs are proceeding well when the damaged pirate ship turns up. Trent and the others hide, then quietly capture the pirates when they board and restore the ship's drive. They make it to another planet where the prisoners are turned over to the authorities and the ship is classified as salvage. The remaining free pirates announce that they will be taking hostages who will only be released in return for their captured shipmates.

Trent, who is now in love with the woman he rescued during the first encounter, is incensed when he discovers that she is probably among the hostages. He has to escape from another pirate ship – this time definitely the privateer gone rogue – by disabling the attacker's drive. From internal evidence left behind by the men he captured, Trent rather implausibly figures out that they are headquartered on an uninhabited world, so he takes his ship there pretending to be another band of pirates. He rescues the hostages and destroys the pirate stronghold, thereby breaking their stranglehold on local interstellar commerce.

Checkpoint Lambda (1966) is a space station in an otherwise uninhabited system which serves as a beacon for starships on various routes. Scott, the protagonist, has been reassigned as station commander, but things start to turn strange shortly before his arrival While en route, Scott hears that a ship that was supposed to pick up passengers and freight was told that neither was there and that the ship should not stop. It is quite clear that the current staff did not want visitors for some reason. Scott is concerned that it involves the imminent arrival of a ship carrying a very valuable cargo. He suspects that criminals have taken over the station in order to steal the treasure.

When they arrive, the station radios orders that no contact is to be made. Scott radios back that he is taking command, and that if they do not let him board, he will commandeer the ship and warn off any other space vessels approaching until a military unit can be summoned. He also notices that no efforts have been made to shift the station in anticipation of the passage of a comet.

Scott is allowed aboard and immediately recognizes that the uniformed men pretending to be crew are actually civilians. He makes it quite clear that he has not been fooled and insists that they retrieve whoever is actually in charge. He then broadcasts an announcement that the station has been allowed to remain on a collision course with at least one comet and that he is not certain whether or not its destruction can be avoided. Everyone on the station would die if that happens.

The boss is a man named Chenery who insists that Scott saved his life once when he was to be executed for a crime that he had not committed. There is a young woman named Janet on the station who is clearly not one of the conspirators. Everyone else – transient passengers and crew - is dead. Scott realizes that Chenery has lost control of his own men, however, and Scott maneuvers things so that the three of them are alone in the control room. The man who has displaced Chenery, Bugsy, does not believe that they are really in danger from the comets and he tries, unsuccessfully, to kill Scott.

Bugsy believes that the danger from the comets is a ruse and that Scott is actually just another crook trying to hijack the heist. Some of his men are nervous anyway because they can actually see the comets approaching. Scott meets with Bugsy again and points out that his astrogator died when they took over the station, so there is no way they could move the treasure ship they are planning to waylay and hijack. They also need a recognition code or the treasure ship would not dock in any case. None of the villains in the novel are particularly bright – they did not even arrange for an alternate method of escape.

Scott keeps his plans to himself, but teaches Janet how to launch and control a lifeboat. Bugsy is finally convinced that the comets will destroy the station if it does not change its orbit. The treasure ship arrives early and Scott quietly warns it off. He somewhat belatedly realizes that Janet can be used against him and he has hidden her elsewhere on the station where she is nevertheless vulnerable.

Fighting breaks out among the thieves and those loyal to Chenery are all killed. Chenery joins Scott and they hold off an attack on the control room. Janet is hiding in a lifeboat but a meteorite hits it and Scott is forced to rescue her. Chenery tries to eliminate Bugsy but is taken captive instead. Scott arranges for the station to be partially sheltered behind an asteroid, but the part where the villains are staying is exposed to a rain of tiny meteorites and they are all killed.

The novel follows the same pattern as *Invaders of Space* and *The Other Side of Nowhere* in that a single honest man has to overcome a large number of criminals, rescuing the innocent young woman in the process. Scott's determination not to kill anyone unless absolutely necessary is not entirely convincing. He ignores two chances to end the takeover and save his own and Janet's life because each would involve at least one fatality – and eventually his actions kill literally all of his enemies anyway. He also places her in jeopardy at one point for no reason at all except to advance the plot.

Space Gypsies (1967) is another space opera. The starship Marintha has a captain named Howell and an engineer named Ketch. Breen is a botanist who is accompanied by his adult daughter Karen. They have been visiting unexplored worlds for some time and have found more traces of a vanished civilization whose cities are all in ruins. It appears that an ancient race wiped out all other intelligences which meant that humans could dominate the galaxy once they reached the required level of civilization.

Howell is therefore quite startled when they emerge from hyperspace and discover a starship not conforming to any human design. The alien ship broadcasts in what is clearly not human speech and they remain silent. Then it switches to an unidentified human tongue and when Karen tries to answer, they are immediately attacked and damaged, although they escape into hyperspace.

They head for an earthlike world in order to make repairs, although their hyperdrive fails again and it looks as though it is a total loss. They are worried that they will be followed because the alien ship obviously knows that they are human and will only have to check each habitable world in the area to find them. As they prepare to land, they pick up an unintelligible recorded message, possibly a distress call, and locate a third type of starship apparently disabled in the midst of a forest.

They land some distance away and Howell advances on foot. He is surprised to find that all plant and animal life surrounding the downed ship has been killed somehow, and alarmed when he discovers that the ship is a mockup, apparently designed as a lure. But there are the skeletons that appear to be three human children nearby. Howell suspects that there are humans living on the planet, but that they are hiding from the aliens.

Howell has the others build several dummies and then arranges them around the lure so that it looks as though they died after tripping a wire that activated a killing field. A day later, they hear one of the alien ships entering the atmosphere. They ambush a party of sluglike creatures in spacesuits, but after killing two, they find themselves under siege by both the landing party and the weapons of the grounded spaceship.

An unknown force destroys the grounded ship, although a second remains in orbit, and the rest of the alien landing party is wiped out. The locals show themselves at last. They are adults but no taller than children, which explains the three skeletons found earlier. Howell determines that the Marintha's engines are not repairable without outside assistance so they appear to be marooned.

They have limited communication but learn that the diminutive humans live in small spaceships rather than cities and that they move around a great deal, hence the title of the novel. It is possible that they may be able to repair the Marintha. Ketch begins to argue with Howell about the best approach. Ketch wants to organize the other humans into a fleet to hunt down the aliens while Howell is more concerned with concealing the existence of Earth, and perhaps returning to it.

Some of the small men work on the Marintha, which eventually launches and successfully enters hyperspace – but finds itself unable to return to normal space. Ketch and Breen have been left behind. The problem is eventually fixed, but they are being trailed by one of the alien ships so they dare not go to Earth or even back to the world of the small men. An alien fleet shows up, but Howell figures out a way to lose them, at least temporarily. He plans to return Karen to her father and then destroy the Marintha so that the aliens cannot find any clues about human civilization.

The small people have been fascinated with the Marintha's garbage disposal system, which dissolves plastic. The aliens are chlorine breathers and their ships have to be coated in plastic to protect the metal components. So they build garbage disposal projectors on their ships which destroy the aliens at a distance, as Howell discovers when he tries the same trick. He recovers his other passengers and heads for home, confident that the aliens will never be able to counter this weapon. The story is relatively minor and has a disappointing deus ex machina ending.

Miners in the Sky (1967) was the last of Leinster's novels other than five television tie-ins. Dunne and Keyes are mining an airless rock in a ring of similar objects in a distant star system. Dunne is on a supply run in their small spacecraft when an attempt is made to ambush him. He drives the attackers away and reaches Outlook, a much larger piece of debris where pickup ships arrive from out of the system and where supplies can be purchased.

Dunne runs into a miner named Smithers who insists that aliens killed his partner. He also finds Keyes' sister Nike, who turns up unexpectedly and insists that it is a matter of life and death that she speak to her brother. Dunne tells her that it is too dangerous to take her to their mine but that he will happily bring a letter. There is also talk of Big Rock Candy Mountain, a legendary rock that contains more riches than are imaginable – and which appears to be the source of the treasure in *Checkpoint Lambda*.

While Dunne is arranging for supplies, someone blows up his spaceship. A miner named Haney offers to transport him in return for half of their find, but Dunne distrusts him. Dunne buys one of the lifeboats from the supply ship, although he has to pressure its captain in order to do so. Predictably the sister stows away until he is too far from the base to turn back. They are trailed by a number of other ships each hoping to jump his claim. Dunne refrains from telling her that since someone destroyed his ship, that party must already know where the mine is.

Dunne drives off the other ships with a small bazooka, but Haney fires back, which indicates that he knows where Dunne is headed and is interested in murder rather than claim jumping. This also suggests to him that Keyes has already been killed. They drift for a while to fool any further pursuit, and during this period their radio picks up a strange sound which Dunne indicates has been heard by other miners before but has never been explained.

They reach the mine and find Keyes dead. There is a booby trap as well, which Dunne safely detonates. They are attempting to mine some more crystals with which to bolster their credit when Smithers shows up in his own ship. He is hunting for the aliens, which has become an obsession. Then Haney arrives and there is an exchange of fire that leaves Dunne and Nike in a damaged life ship which has lost its air.

Their space drive is damaged and they travel out of control for a considerable distance before Dunne can make repairs. He has been thinking about the chain of events and now speculates that Haney is motivated by the desire to kill Nike rather than Dunne. The explanation is that Nike and her brother were heirs to a fortune found by their uncle, Joe Griffiths. But the legal case has not been completed and if the two of them die before the final judgment, the estate passes to a cousin, who happens to be married to Haney.

Smithers has been broadcasting warnings to other miners that Haney is killing people and stealing their finds. Dunne and Nike decide to hide behind a large rock fragment and discover that it is Big Rock Candy Mountain. Haney tries to kill them with a bazooka but instead sets off a chain reaction that permanently blinds him. Dunne brings him back to the supply station and he and Nike go off to collect the legacy. As a postscript, we learn that aliens are in fact present in the system, but they are so horrified by the violence they have seen that they vow never to contact humanity again.

The Time Tunnel (1967) was the first of two tie-in novels to the television series, which ran for one season 1966-1967. Two scientists are lost in time as the result of a secret government time travel project, which is trying to bring them back to the present. Some episodes were set in the past, others in the future. The book starts with a variation of the first episode, in order to set up the premise.

Tony Newman is escorting Senator Clark to a demonstration of the secret project where he works with Doug Phillips. Clark has no idea what the project is about and he is irritated at the level of secrecy. When told that it is an attempt to develop time travel, he has two objections. First of all, he believes that it is completely impossible. Second, if it was possible, it would be incredibly dangerous because of the risk that a change in the past would wipe out the present. The scientists – and the author – talk around the second objection without really addressing it. Clark announces that he will expose the project and have it stopped.

Newman decides to be the first human to test the tunnel. He finds himself in the unknown past – there is apparently no way to calibrate the transfer – but has a radio that is somehow capable of communicating with the present. The initial attempt to bring him back fails and he decides to explore, spying on a group of men who are trying to raise the height of a small dam. He finds a newspaper from 1889 and discovers that he is in Johnstown, Pennsylvania, just in time for its famous flood.

Newman struggles with the temptation to try to help, knowing that would change history. He decides that he cannot be brought back to the present because historically he already did something in the past and he must complete that act before the tunnel will work again. He turns off his communication device and starts toward town, trying to warn people along the way. Predictably, no one pays any attention to him.

Phillips decides to go through the tunnel and bring Newman back. Newman has been detained as mentally disturbed and Phillips pretends to be his doctor. The flood hits and after some efforts to help, the two men are snatched back through time after saving Senator Clark's grandmother. But they fail to return to the present. From what they can see, they decide they are somewhere in the Great Plains region late in the 19th Century.

A party of hostile Comanches shows up but they are apparently frightened because of the strange clothing worn by the time travelers. They are picked up by some freight wagons who are accompanied by an armed escort. They reach an outpost which history says will be attacked by hostile Comanches quite soon, and that Bat Masterson was among the defenders.

The attack comes as expected and the time travelers are caught inside the besieged outpost. They survive, of course, and the next jump in time takes them to a futuristic city for a brief visit. The city is deserted but they find news accounts of a force field covering the area that was apparently established by hostile aliens. They return to the present at last where they decide to use time travel to guide humanity to a more benevolent future. The premise is littered with flaws, but Leinster had limited ability to alter the parameters of the television program.

Timeslip! (1967) was the second Time Tunnel novel. The initial premise is not very plausible. A nuclear missile is to be sent back into time, then brought forward into the present at another location, thus proving that an attack could be launched that would be undetectable. There is, of course, no reason why an actual missile would have to be used in a test. Nor for it to be conducted by people without a working knowledge of the equipment.

In any case, the experiment goes awry and the missile is lost in Mexico City in 1847, buried out of sight beneath a small lake. Unfortunately a construction project in the present is working in the same area and might set off the missile at any moment. This is also problematic since nuclear missiles are not set off by impact. In any case, an expedition into the past is planned to retrieve the missile. They reach the lake without incident even though the US Army has just invaded Mexico.

The missile must be dried before it can be placed in a harness and brought back to its original time period. One member of the team, Sam Creighton, encounters a soldier who turns out to be one of his ancestors. They make a slight change to history but are able to correct it by impersonation and subterfuge. Leinster uses the conflict to describe some of the unethical and illegal activities pursued by the American soldiers during the war. The bomb is eventually retrieved successfully amidst some arguing about whether or not the project should be shut down.

Leinster ended his career with three novels based on the *Land of the Giants* television show. This show ran for two seasons, 1968-1970, and involved a space shuttle that encounters some kind of anomaly and travels to another planet which is basically Earth, except that everything is twelve times as large. There were inconsistencies in the series as well as gross scientific inaccuracies. The physical impossibility of bipeds as large as giants is alluded to but not addressed.

Land of the Giants (1968, aka *The Trap*) changes the set-up slightly to make it somewhat more realistic. Steve Burton is pilot of the Spindrift, a high altitude passenger ship. Dan Ericson is part of the crew. Betty Hamilton is the stewardess. Both men have been warned to be very careful because of reports of a space warp in Earth's orbit. These reports caused most of the passengers to cancel their flights and only four are aboard when they take off.

Predictably, they encounter the warp and all of their communications and most other equipment fails. They find themselves orbiting an unknown but earthlike planet and are able to land. Within minutes, they see a gigantic vehicle pass by and realize that they are no longer in scale with their environment.

Much of the novel consists of them sneaking around and spying on the planet's inhabitants, who are giant humans. One of the passengers is a young boy named Barry who has a dog, and a slightly older young woman named Valerie. Fitzhugh and Wilson are both adult males. Fitzhugh is obstreperous and lazy. Valerie and Barry run into a box trap and Valerie is carried off by one of the giants.

Dan sneaks into the giant's house and frees Valerie, but they both have to hide when two more giants appear. Another woman is also imprisoned there, but they are initially unable to help her. The seven humans decide to rescue the unknown woman, but Fitzhugh disappears along the way, apparently terrified. They start several fires to distract the giants, then free the woman, Marjorie, who was a passenger on another ship that passed through the warp.

Some minor adventures – giant puppies and bats – follow before they learn that the giants have a slightly more advanced technology than humans. Although they do not use radio. The fugitives move the Spindrift to a remote area, where they secretly observe a party of giants hunting birds. They are able to forage for food and an examination of the sky suggests they are eleven light years from Earth, but that they have not moved in time.

The giants have a device that nullifies their engines, but activation of their radio nullifies the device. Fitzhugh continues to complain and act unwisely enough to place them all in jeopardy. They attempt to find another space warp to take them home, but as the book ends, they are still trapped and fugitives. The giants are aware of them, obviously, but it is also hinted that they were responsible for the space warp in the first place.

The Hot Spot (1969) briefly reprises events in the first book. Burton decides to land on a remote island and maintain radio silence so that the giants will think that they are gone. Burton still maintains that there is a chance they can return to Earth, although the circumstances make this wildly unlikely. Shortly after landing, they see a monstrous spider and soon other oversized insects are making life complicated and dangerous.

They spend the night quietly but in the morning a spiderweb covers the ship, and it is strong enough that they cannot safely take off again. Although this sequence is reminiscent of *The Forgotten Planet*, it lacks the inventiveness of that much earlier work. The men manage to kill a pair of spiders, mostly with axes since there were no weapons aboard except for a single handgun. The ship is still trapped, although they are working on freeing it. The giants for some reason have never developed air travel, but there are hunting parties in the area and they have boats.

Some of the humans manage to sneak aboard one of the oversized boats where they have to deal with the ship's cat. While the hunters are dealing with oversized turtles, the Spindrift is moved to the ship's relatively stable deck. They successfully take off when everyone is aboard, but an air leak nearly causes a disaster. They outwit some robot airships and find a new place to hide. There is no explanation of why the giants would have unmanned airships only.

They land near a farm, which they raid to replenish their food supplies. Several of them are temporarily trapped inside one of the farm buildings, but they escape without much difficulty. The ship takes off again and Burton's equipment suggests that a new space warp is forming, so they head in that direction, hoping to finally find a way home.

Unknown Danger (1969) was the third and last in the series published in the US – there were two additional titles by James Bradwell in the UK. It was also Leinster's last published novel. Burton is now convinced that they were purposely abducted although he has no idea why. The Spindrift is experiencing more mechanical problems and they have limited ability to make repairs. The space warp sighted at the end of the previous book is not functioning as they had hoped. When they emerge, they are still above the giant world.

They find themselves over an immense ocean and when they approach a giant whose fishing boat is sinking, he throws things at them in a fury. Another ship carrying rockets begins firing at a school of porpoise and Burton takes their own ship under the water for safety. Later they go ashore on an island and are attacked by a giant carrying an energy weapon.

Burton decides to confuse things by faking a radio conversation, suggesting that there are two ships rather than one. Any attempt to communicate with the giants is met with instant hostility. In fact it appears that the giants are preparing large batteries of rockets to use against them. Some minor adventures follow before they make a trip to one of the planet's two moons and sabotage the power generation equipment there by dropping large rocks from orbit. This limits the ability of the giants to attack them, but still does not provide a way back to Earth.

SHORT SCIENCE FICTION

Most of Leinster's best science fiction can be found among his short stories. The first of these appeared as early as 1918 and his first real science fiction was "The Runaway Skyscraper" (1919), which was the first in the Preston-Hines series. Most of the early stories – including jungle tales, mysteries, and other genres - appeared in *Argosy, Colliers, Jungle Tales*, and elsewhere and unfortunately they remain largely unavailable.

"The Runaway Skyscraper" was the first of four stories, the other three of which have never been collected. Arthur Chamberlain is a struggling young engineer who notices one day that the nearby clock tower has begun to run backward. In fact his entire building is going backward through time at an accelerated pace as the result of some unusual natural disaster. It comes to rest near a Native American village thousands of years before Columbus.

There is a residual vibration that Chamberlain believes will provide a way for them to eventually return, but there are two thousand people in the building and they have less than a day's worth of food. Hunting and fishing are organized but the scale is inadequate to the demand and many of the people are either apathetic or panic stricken. Eventually Chamberlain solves the problem and they all return to their original time.

Although the story is fun, it contains several contradictions. Time is apparently running normally inside the building, yet wristwatches are also running in reverse. It is somewhat in advance of its time in that the only female character, Chamberlain's secretary, is a competent person who actually contributes significantly to their survival.

"A Thousand Degrees Below Zero" (1919) was the first of two stories about Gerrod, a scientist, and Davis, a pilot, who save the world from a mad scientist. One hot day in August, New York's harbor mysteriously freezes solid. A message from someone named Varrhus demands the surrender of the entire planet to his rule and threatens to use the same method to freeze all the waterways of the world. Varrhus is apparently piloting a revolutionary new kind of aircraft.

Teddy Gerrod works with elderly Professor Hawkins and figures out that the ice is being formed by a process of heat exchange. Firing explosives near the center of the process disrupts it successfully. But a few days later several widely dispersed bodies of water begin to freeze simultaneously. The process has been changed to disguise the vulnerable area. Varrhus also arranges for the murder of Professor Hawkins.

With the aid of Davis, Gerrod ambushes Varrhus' aircraft, but it is invulnerable to their weaponry and he escapes. Efforts to counter the new configurations of the ice bombs have limited success. Gerrod comes up with a new plan and this time they disable the mystery ship and Varrhus is killed. The frozen areas can now be cleared and the world is saved.

Gerrod and Davis returned in "The Silver Menace" (1919). This time a natural disaster causes the problem. A yacht finds itself suddenly immovable despite having its engines in perfect condition. The water itself has become thickened and turned the color of silver. As the phenomenon spreads, virtually all ocean travel comes to a standstill. Gerrod and David fly to the yacht where the former discovers that the problem consists of tiny life forms that merge into jellylike masses. Even worse, the creatures begin to spread across dry land as well. Eventually Gerrod discovers that a certain sound wave kills the creatures and the world is saved again.

"The Darkness on Fifth Avenue" (1929) was not about the stock market crash. Police Lieutenant Hines just happens to be in a city park when a criminal named Dunn tries a new device, one which can project a cloud of utter darkness over a limited area. The mobsters shoot a man almost in front of Hines and make their escape. The wounded man is a scientist who was working with Preston, the inventor of the darkness device. Preston has developed a way to work in the darkness and Dunn's gang pulls off a series of robberies while leaving the police powerless to interfere. A trap is laid in which the next wave of darkness is surrounded by fire trucks pumping water into the area. The cordon moves with the darkness and eventually the batteries powering the device fail and he and Dunn are both killed. Although the science is dubious, this was a successful problem story.

"The Fifth-Dimensional Catapult" (1931) is the first adventure of Tommy Reames, an unlikely young scientist who receives a telegram indicating that his article on human perception of space and time has put the life of another scientist in jeopardy. He arrives to find that Professor Denham and his daughter Evelyn were conducting an experiment and became marooned in the fifth dimension, leaving only his assistant, Von Holtz, behind.

Reames is able to use a kind of telescope to see Denham and his surroundings, which are vaguely Jurassic, although in the distance he can see what appears to be a city. Denham's assistant tells him that they have seen people he calls the Ragged Men in the area and that they will kill the intruders if they find them. The Ragged Men are primitive humans who obviously hate the city dwellers.

Reames agrees to try to effect a rescue, but he also discovers that Von Holtz sabotaged the capsule so that Denham could not return and is working with someone else to steal his secrets. Von Holtz also mentions a man named Jacaro who helped finance Denham's experiments, but whom the reader knows is the mobster who bribed Von Holtz.

Reames enlists the aid of a mechanic named Smithers. When it is obvious that Reames has figured out how to replicate Denham's work, Von Holtz threatens him and Jacaro tries to bribe him. Smithers smuggles in a machine gun with some supplies but rather oddly no one attempts to contact the authorities. Reames creates a new device to travel between dimensions, then watches as the Ragged Men attack and kill all but one member of a group from the city. They take the last man captive. Denham and his daughter try to help and they are captured as well.

Reames uses the device to allow Smithers to shoot his machine gun into the other dimension and kill many of the Ragged Men. The city man is killed but the two explorers escape. Unfortunately, the city sends a wave of poison gas in their direction and while Reames is trying to deal with that, Jacaro's gunmen attack and Smithers is shot. He manages to pull Denham and Evelyn back into their original dimension, but Jacaro's men steal the device, leaving a cliffhanger ending.

The story is similar in structure to the journeys inside atoms in the early stories of Ray Cummings, although the prose is much better and the attempt to rationalize the process — although still scientifically nonsense — is much more detailed. Tommy Reames would return in "The Fifth-Dimension Tube" (1932).

Working with Denham, Reames creates a more practical method

of visiting the other dimension, determined to thwart Jacaro's efforts to exploit that civilization, in which gold is a common element. The reader can interpolate his activities from the fact that a giant lizard was killed when it attacked some cattle, and jewelry stores have been puzzled by an influx of precious gems which has reduced the value of their stock. The Tube is a kind of tunnel through which people can pass back and forth to the other dimension with relative ease.

Jacaro has disappeared. There are reports of poisonous fogs and Reames speculates that the city people in the other world are sending the poison back through Jacaro's Tube. Reames and Smithers rescue Von Holtz, who is being pursued by a band of Ragged Men. He tells them that Jacaro's Tube terminates inside the city, that the gangsters had stolen jewels and other items and had killed some of the local people. Then a major fight and explosion prevented them from returning to the Tube and they had fled the city. Because they were seen fighting with the city people, the Ragged Men had given them shelter.

Reames and Evelyn go through the tube and she is promptly carried off by a dinosaur. He manages to rescue her but they are far away from the Tube by then. The Ragged Men attack the Tube and may have rendered it useless in any case. When they reach it, they can talk to Smithers but cannot travel back. The poison gas is still coming through Jacaro's Tube, the location of which is unknown.

Reames and Evelyn manage to evade the Ragged Men, but are attacked by a flying vehicle from the city. They wound its pilot and capture the vehicle. A truce of sorts is reached and the pilot takes them to the city, which is strangely unpopulated. They learn the local language and speak to the governing council, but to their horror they discover that the world is becoming less habitable and the city people plan to use the gas to wipe out the human race so that they can take over the planet.

A rival city launches an attack and Reames helps drive off the invaders. Denham and Smithers come through Jacaro's Tube to join them, after which it is destroyed to prevent the transfer of more poison gas. The war escalates with Jacaro helping the enemy city and our heroes helping the other. Evelyn is captured.

The war ends with the defeat of the attackers and the death of Jacaro. Evelyn is rescued. Plans to invade the Earth are cancelled. The visitors are stranded there, but decide they are not unhappy with the situation. The sequel has a much livelier plot and shows us more about the other world, but the sense of mystery and wonder is not as prevalent.

"Morale: A Story of the War of 1941-1943" (1931) takes place with the United States at war with an unnamed enemy, although the fighting is initially confined to the West Coast. A surprise attack on the East Coast consists of the landing of a single supertank – two hundred feet in length – which would eventually be known as a Wabbly. Its primary purpose was to undermine the morale of the local population. Armed with gas shells and a kind of heat ray, guarded by a fleet of aircraft, it appears invulnerable until two soldiers manage to destroy it by trickery. A very minor story and far too long for its content. Vaguely resembling "The Land Ironclads" by H.G. Wells.

"The Power Planet" may have seemed plausible at the time, but the science does not stand up to present day scrutiny. The title refers to an artificial satellite that beams power to Earth. The crew is an international one and – for no apparent reason except to establish the situation – radio communication with Earth is impossible. So when the crew realizes that nuclear war has broken out on Earth, no one knows who is on which side. A rocket is on its way to either destroy or seize the Power Planet, and early attempts to attack the rocket before it arrives all fail. Eventually the defenders find a way to defeat the enemy, which also sets the stage for establishing remote shielding to protect friendly cities on Earth. The story is almost unreadable and is one of Leinster's least effective efforts.

"Politics" (1932) it is also a war story – future war stories were very popular at the time, and also quite cynical. This time it is a naval battle in the Pacific against another unidentified enemy. Most of the American fleet has been destroyed and the survivors largely blame the disaster on political shortcomings which have hampered their operations. The rather implausible explanation is that the main fleet was ordered to avoid serious contact with the enemy until after the current elections, and this led to their destruction by a more aggressive foe.

The Minnesota is the most powerful battleship in the world and it has new range finders that make it the most accurate. Unfortunately, pacifists want the country to surrender. The military is determined to go down fighting even if that means disobeying orders. The political situation as described is not really credible – it is hard to imagine a scenario in which the country would be swept by pacifism, particularly during the 1930s. The enemy fleet is destroyed thanks to the new range finders and the result is that pacifism is refuted and the military is declared no longer subject to civilian control – which is never justified or explained and would be positively dangerous to democratic rule.

"Borneo Devils" (1933) opens with reports that diminutive winged devils are abducting people in Borneo. A party of explorers is attacked by them and they manage to kill one before discovering that much of their ammunition has been replaced with soft shells that are unlikely to do much damage. A mysterious human figure appears to be controlling the creatures. The explanation is a partial rationalization. They are actually hornbilled storks who have been addicted to a drug, trained to attack, and have had their bills smeared with poison. Science fiction only in the most minimal sense.

"Invasion" (1933) is a very dated, highly improbable story in which the communist nations fake a Martian invasion of the United States in order to erect force fields over all of the defense installations and allow a conventional attack against an undefended nation. The hero and his girlfriend are caught inside the main force dome and are held prisoner by a comic book style villain until they disable him with a slingshot and turn off the force fields, thereby saving the country.

"Sidewise in Time" (1934) was Leinster's first excellent short story. It is one of the classic stories of alternate worlds, and it gave the name to the Sidewise Awards given for that subgenre. A series of bizarre events sweeps over the world. Vikings appear on a local river and loot a town. A dinosaur eats a farmer. A salesman finds himself in the Confederate States of America. Apparently time and probability have come unglued. The idea that decision points generate different futures was established with this story, the bulk of which consists of anecdotes about anomalous confrontations.

There is, however, a central plot. A professor named Minott has figured out what is wrong. He forcibly recruits a handful of bright students and leads them on a search for a world where they can establish themselves as rulers by means of their greater knowledge of science. Minott's party breaks up and most return to their original world. The shifting of time and probability comes to an end with the

Earth restored, almost, to its original state. Although there is not much of an actual unifying plot, this was an innovative story that is now rightly considered a genre classic.

"The Mole Pirate" (1934) is in large part a duel of wits between Jack Hill, a scientist, and James Durran, a wanted criminal and also a scientist. Hill has developed a way to affect atoms so that one solid object can pass through another. He is about to demonstrate it when the device – the Mole - is stolen by Durran. Durran visits an armory for weapons and a prison to recruit allies. He begins robbing banks and the only ways to stop him are costly – radioactive bullets or specially prepared vaults. Hill is working on a newer and faster vehicle, but Durran destroys the construction site.

Various attempts to stop the Mole have limited success. Durran tries to kill Hill but fails, though a second attempt leaves Hill a captive. Durran sets Hill free in exchange for the locations of the new ships under construction, but he holds his girlfriend hostage. She is later released in return for a ransom, but Hill has found a way to wear out the substance that prevents the Mole from sliding into the Earth and it falls to the planet's core. Although the science is nonsense, the solution to the problem given the premise is reasonable and convincing.

"Proxima Centauri" (1935) is the story of humanity's first trip to another star, by means of a massive ship that travels below the speed of light. The two chief officers are somewhat suspicious of one member of the crew, Jack Gary, because he is a Mut, a former mutineer, but the captain's daughter believes they are being unfair. They mutiny took place in the third year of the voyage when boredom and dissatisfaction led to segregation of the officers from the rest of the crew, who were controlled by force of arms.

They begin to receive signals from their destination which are designed to look like they are being sent from a planet. In fact, there is another spaceship coming to meet them and their first encounter suggests that the aliens are hostile. The alien ship is apparently made from organic matter and there is an immediate attack against the human ship with radiation designed to kill everyone aboard, although it is not powerful enough to pass through the reinforced hull. A boarding party is ambushed and the creatures are revealed to be halfway between plant and animal. They prize animal flesh as though it was gold, and the humans decide that there is no possibility of peaceful relations.

An alien fleet shows up and their combined firepower is sufficient to begin melting the hull, but the humans are able to communicate well enough to indicate that they have peaceful intentions and the attack is suspended with their effective surrender. The ship's captain dies and the second in command takes over. He is forced to allow another alien party aboard and most of the humans are killed almost immediately. Jack Gary and the captain's daughter are sent to a pastoral planet as personal property of one of the leading aliens. Conveniently, virtually the entire race has remained on its home planet and all of its spaceships have landed when the new captain detonates the ship's engines, which causes a chain reaction and destroys the entire species. The two survivors are alone to make their new future. This story and "Sidewise in Time" were the first indications of the flurry of superior short stories Leinster would produce over the course of the rest of his career.

The protagonist of "The Fourth-Dimensional Demonstrator" (1935) has just inherited an estate from his uncle, an expert on the fourth dimension, but there seem to be more debts than assets. There is also a machine which brings items forward out of time to the present, effectively duplicating them. But when paper money is duplicated, every bill has the same serial number, which leads to charges of counterfeiting. The protagonist's obnoxious girlfriend inadvertently makes multiple copies of herself, along with her pet kangaroo. The humor is not particularly realistic, but it develops logically from the situation.

"The Wabbler" (1942) is not really a story. It is an account of a cybernetic device that is dropped into the ocean, penetrates a submarine net, enters a harbor, and destroys an enemy vessel. "If You Can Get It" (1943) is also very minor. A researcher figures out a way to perform what is effectively magic and transports himself to an ideal world, but when he returns to ours, he forgets how to get back.

"Plague" (1944) pokes fun at bureaucracies. The government of human colonized space is moribund with forms, regulations, and incompetent bureaucrats. Ben Sholto is ordered to use his personal spaceship to help enforce the quarantine on a planet affected by an alien plague. A ship defies the quarantine and is scheduled to be destroyed, but Sholto discovers that Sally Hale, the love of his life, is aboard.

The plague only affects women and she believed she had not been exposed and fled. Sholto tries to fake her death in space but his plans go awry. Hale begins to show symptoms of the plague, but then they stop and Sholto realizes that there is an alien life form on the ship that briefly inhabited her body and then left. It returns, however, and she will die in a matter of days if it remains. Hiding from the authorities inside a belt of meteors, they find a way to drive the creature out of her body. They are apprehended by a military ship, so Sholto infects its crew in order to blackmail them into not killing him. Fortunately, the female head of the government becomes one of those possessed and she is sensible enough to pardon Sholto and Hale and take effective steps to counteract the alien infestation and save the day.

"Trog" (1944) is a slightly overlong story about the difficulties of dealing with a post collapse world that was created because humanity's unsuspected mass consciousness rebelled against civilization and caused countless bits of sabotage to bring it all to an end. In "The Eternal Now" (1984) a group of people are trapped in a frozen moment in time after a scientific experiment goes awry. The scientific explanation of how they escape is doubletalk, but the imagery of the world frozen in time is hauntingly effective.

"De Profundis" (1945) is one of those stories narrated by an alien that is similar to some of the best work of Hal Clement. The narrator lives at the bottom of Earth's oceans and his race – tentacled and enormous - has created a theory of the universe that assumes it is filled from end to end with water. When he is able to eavesdrop on the thoughts of two people trapped in a sunken bathyscaphe, he carries it back to the surface, but his fellow beings assume that he was delusional about the nature of humans and the possibility of life inside a cloud of gas.

"First Contact" (1945) is Leinster's best known short story and the second whose title became a common genre term, in this case referring to stories of the initial meeting between humans and another intelligent race. It is also an excellent example of the problem story, i.e., one in which the focus of the plot is the solution to some sort of physical or logical quandary. It won one of Leinster's two Hugo awards for best novelette.

An exploratory ship from Earth encounters a similar one from the first space traveling race humanity has ever encountered. Neither can trust the other because it is possible that one side or the other is aggressive. Neither can go home without risking that the other will monitor their progress and identify their home world. The aliens exchange information through a form of telepathy and with computers the two ships are able to establish a means of communication, though neither knows if the other side is telling the truth. The ultimate solution is that each refits the other's ship to suit their needs and both return to their respective home worlds in the other's vessel, with a promise to meet at a neutral site in the future. Although somewhat simplistic and dependent upon coincidental similarities, the premise and resolution were quite original when the story was published.

"The Ethical Equations" (1945) is another first contact story. A junior officer on a spaceship notices an anomalous object and raises a stink until political pressure forces his captain to temporarily cede command while it is investigated. He finds a derelict spaceship, its crew in suspended animation, clearly almost out of fuel. Despite demands that he permit the ship to be taken to Earth for further examination, he insists that it be studied but not touched, and eventually determines that some of its components would react explosively with elements which are common in the solar system. He refuels the ship and sends it back toward its home world to demonstrate that humans are not hostile. The title refers to a vaguely explained theory that ethics must also achieve a form of balance. "Adapter" (1946) is a far inferior sequel about contact with an alternate universe.

"Tight Place" (1945) is a minor problem story in which two men find themselves drifting in space after a battle and have to cooperate if they are to reach safety. "Pipeline to Pluto" (1945) is a revenge story about a man sent on what should have been a fatal attempt at stowing away in space but who returns and traps the men responsible, forcing them to undergo the same ordeal. An alien stranded on Earth is believed to be a supernatural being in "The Power" (1945).

"Things Pass By" (1945) opens with a warning that a fleet of gigantic alien ships is going to pass close enough to Earth to disrupt our gravity and destroy humanity even though it is unintentional. Two cosmoquakes will strike the Earth causing gravitational anomalies that will kill millions of people, and this is just from the advance scouts. The main body will destroy the Earth when it comes close enough.

The story then shifts to Dirk Braddick, a scientist who is surprised to discover that a young woman has parachuted into his high security compound. He suspects she is an industrial spy but she is suffering from partial amnesia. He calls her Jane and appoints her as his temporary assistant, then makes a deal with the evil corporation. They are to send a technician to help him build a spaceship using a new technique he has developed. The technician is accompanied by a thug who reacts with aggressive hostility when he sees Jane.

The ship is launched despite an inexplicable bombing attack by the rival corporation. Jane recovers her memory – she is the actual legal owner of the corporation but has been held incommunicado. Braddick finds a way to redirect the oncoming fleet and save Earth, but the solution is mostly scientific doubletalk and it is the interplay among the characters that is the point of the story. He has to defeat the thug along the way and ultimately becomes engaged to Jane. Although it is a fairly good story, the ending is disappointing and abrupt.

"Incident on Calypso" (1945), another first contact story, opens with the protagonist landing on Callisto. His ship malfunctioned and he is marooned there with no way to call for help and only enough air to last for a few days. Out of curiosity he investigates what appear to be footprints and finds three dormant robots, one of which he carries back to his ship. He revives it and develops a limited ability to communicate with its processor. The robot then revives its fellows, who were stranded just as he was, but they can use what is left of the human ship's fuel more efficiently and escape. They build him a new space drive so that he can do the same.

"Interference" (1945) is a minor story that is not quite about time travel. An investigation concerning television interference reveals a time portal and a dead man. It turns out that the portal connects to neither the future or the past but to a parallel world, and it ends without any actual climax. "The Plants" (1946) opens with the crash landing of a ship on a planet populated only by a single life form, a flowering plant. One member of the crew sabotaged the ship for reasons unknown and left it in a lifeboat and only four men survive the crash. They conclude that the saboteur was meeting another ship and that they plan to loot the wreck for its cargo. The thieves arrive but the plants have the ability to control minds. They immobilize the pirates and allow the first crew to leave in their ship.

"A Logic Named Joe" (1946) is one of Leinster's most famous stories. The narrator is a service technician for logics, which are a kind of home computer connected to a kind of internet. Although the details differ, the results are so close to reality that the story is one of the most prophetic in all of science fiction. Joe is a logic who, through some error in manufacturing, became self aware.

Joe decides to offer new services to humans that were not previously available, like detailed instructions about how to get away with murder. Some advice is positively useful but some involves theft and other crimes. Chaos reigns until the technician figures out which logic is responsible and turns it off. It ends up hidden in his basement while he speculates about how this development might someday be made safe.

"Dead City" (1946, aka "The Malignant Marauder") sets up an apparent paradox. An archaeologist finds a stainless steel knife that is eight thousand years old and made of an alloy unknown to modern science. He then returns to the Yucatan to further excavate the site and turns up ruins of a pre-Mayan civilization the right age, but the other artifacts do not support the level of technology necessary to have produced the knife.

After examining topological maps, the expedition moves to another site and finds more of the knives, which were clearly mass produced, although their handles are a bit oddly shaped for human hands. Eventually they find the remnants of some kind of ground vehicle, buried for 20,000 years, not designed for human passengers and decorated with a kind of artwork that suggests violence. That night, they feel a vibration that the workers dismiss as a small earthquake.

The scientists begin to suspect that the nearby lake is a bomb crater. Some of the workers spot a shiny object hovering over the lake, but it disappears almost immediately. Further examples of artwork suggest that the residents of the city were able to perceive objects through time as well as space. The shiny object reappears and is presumed to be some kind of time machine. The crew consists of aliens who cannot even breathe Earth's air.

The aliens turn one of the workers into an organic translating device and indicate that they are devoid of emotions themselves, so make use of human emotions instead. They plan to build a new city on the ruins of the old one and then bring the bulk of their race forward through time. One of the men fashions a booby trap when the aliens confiscate their equipment. They take it back through time where it triggers a chain reaction that creates the lake and destroys their domed city, killing everyone within in. The story is very well constructed and is reminiscent of the author's earlier jungle stories.

"The End" (1946) takes place at the literal end of the universe. The galaxies are colliding and destroying themselves. Earth has long been cold and abandoned but a small group of scientists comes back just as it appears that they have less than five years to live. Ron Hort has given up hope but one of the others has found an ancient technology which he insists provides the key to surviving. But at that precise moment, a pirate ship appears and demands the surrender of the entire staff. A handful of people escape to the outpost where the artifact is determined to be capable of negating space itself, thereby allowing it to somehow escape the impending catastrophe by creating a pocket universe. There is a fight with the pirates before the secret is discovered. The survivors are safe in the pocket universe and because of a time differential, when they emerge an entirely new inhabitable universe has been created.

"Skit-Tree Planet" (1947) is a story of planetary exploration. The crew of the Galloping Cow have found a planet that is clearly some kind of artificial farm, although there are no signs of civilization or even animal life. One of their aircraft spots something very large moving in the distance. The plants, skit-trees, have shown up on other planets as well. They spot a distant city, even photograph it, but it disappears when they approach. The city does the same vanishing act several times before they are able to get close to it, and then they are suddenly trapped inside some kind of metal container. They theorize that the aliens project all their artifacts as force fields and turn them off when they are no longer needed. Then a materialized monster destroys their starship. They trace the projection back to its origin, a single alien who survived a plague that destroyed his race. The alien is killed but the humans figure out the technology and create/project a new ship for themselves, which looks like a giant galloping cow.

In "Propagandist" (1947) a malevolent race has been attacking human ships and colonies without provocation. The protagonist is aboard one of the ships seeking to locate the enemy's home world. They find an intelligent race with interplanetary travel and try to decide whether or not these are the ones responsible. The aliens themselves have actually been attacked by the unknowns and are worried that the spaceship they have detected presages another catastrophic event. A landing party is briefly on their planet with no contact, but they inadvertently leave a dog. The aliens are able to get a good idea of human nature from the dog's memories and this leads to an alliance.

"The Day of the Deepies" (1947) is set in a future where science is outlawed and technology is slowly regressing. The deepies are displaced persons, homeless since the war and usually afraid of settling down anywhere. They are the most stridently opposed to science. A meeting has been convened to convince a young man to give up his plans to learn science but it is interrupted by a deepie who announces that a plane has landed nearby. The presence of an airplane is supposed to be a sure sign that the community will be bombed out of existence to suppress scientific knowledge. The deepie – actually an agent of the people keeping a stranglehold on technology – seizes the plane because it is more advanced than anything his people have and flies away with it. Only then do we learn that it was a trick. The plane will explode when it is studied. The local communities are all planning to restore the use of electricity and wanted to prove that they can strike back. The sentiment is admirable but the story is unconvincing.

"Symbiosis" (1947) posits a nation that has infected itself with a deadly disease along with a substance that makes it symbiotic rather than fatal. This causes an invading army to begin dying in large numbers. The consequences of the story are not well thought out since this would necessarily result in a complete quarantine of the country and trade and travel would both be problematic. "Friends" is a rather bad story about telepathic devices that enable two men to avert a war. "Time to Die" (1947) concerns a convicted murderer who mentally travels back in time to try to prevent his being caught, but he only makes things worse for himself.

"Planet of Sand" (1948) begins with Stan Buckley confined in a starship's brig, falsely accused by his supervisor, Rob Torren, because both men are in love with the same woman. The agree to meet on an uninhabited planet for a duel, but the planet consists almost entirely of sand laid over a featureless landscape, except for an obviously artificial maze of columns and roofing that extends for hundreds of miles. There is no plant or animal life, but somehow the atmosphere is breathable.

The maze is automated so that it shifts position periodically and sheds the stand deposited by daily sandstorms. Buckley needs to survive for three months until Torren is able to join him, and that seems unlikely given the circumstances. Thanks to a really incredible coincidence, a small spaceship crashes on the planet hours later, and its sole occupant is Esther Hume, the woman the two men are fighting over. The two of them use small personal fliers to reach the northern pole, where they find tracks from the passage of something gigantic.

They return to the wrecked ship, after excavating some of the sand that now covers it. They use the ship's meteor repellers to turn sand into flying missiles that disable some of the machines, which are operated by an ancient underground civilization. Torren shows up and tries to kill them both, but the aliens emerge and manage to destroy his ship. Buckley, meanwhile, has salvaged parts from the disabled machines and repairs Esther's ship so that they can escape into space.

Although the story has an interesting premise, the execution is sometimes awkward. The coincidences are beyond plausibility. Since someone has surveyed the planet – it was listed as having a breathable atmosphere – why did they fail to report the gigantic artificial anomaly? The assumption that the two people could survive for months by planting seeds is not credible given the time required to grow the plants. When they try to tap into the power system of the maze, they are attacked by giant machines which appear at various points all over the planet, one of them destroying the garden they had planted. The solution assumes a degree of compatibility between technologies that is astronomically unlikely.

The six-fingered protagonist of "The Strange Case of John Kingman" (1948) has been in a mental hospital for years. A new doctor is puzzled by his lack of any documented history and the absence of any record of treatment. Further investigation reveals that Kingman has been a patient for more than a century. A physical examination reveals that he has extra ribs, two hearts, and other indications that he is not a human being. He also displays an immediate understanding of equipment he has never seen before. The doctor assumes that he is an alien, but that he is paranoid by human standards. News reaches the government that Kingman has knowledge of advanced technology – he has been drawing processes and devices that are far in advance of anything on Earth – and locks down the building until the matter can be investigated further. An attempt is made to cure him using a new regimen of drugs, but he has an adverse reaction that changes his personality. Although cured of his paranoia, he now has amnesia and is no longer of any use to the authorities.

"West Wind" (1948) is another war story involving unidentified nations. Igor is hiding in a zone evacuated by one country that refused to defend its territory from an aggressive neighbor. A faction within his government wants him to broadcast coverage of the imminent occupation to shame their countrymen and embarrass their political rivals. Igor, however, is taken prisoner by one of the enemy's advance scouts who wants the truth about some vague threats made against the occupation force. The smaller country then disperses radioactive dust into the air so that it blows toward the army, effectively killing them all. This was a variation of "Symbiosis," and shares both its virtues and its faults.

"Regulations" (1948) has a villain as protagonist, which was unusual for Leinster. Fahnes and Boles have spent several months on an obscure planet trading with the natives. Fahnes plans to maroon his partner and leave with all their goods when the time is right. Trading rules for the planet indicate that no interference with the local religion was allowed. The natives, a kind of oversized insect, abhor the color red and have made it taboo. They also forbid killing. Fahnes violates a taboo by entering their village, where he burns down several houses to cause confusion while he loots their temple. Instead he falls into a holy pool and drowns. Ironically, the natives would have given him the jewels he wanted, and they were relatively worthless zircons rather than diamonds.

"The Devil of East Lupton" (1948) starts with a tramp trying to escape a policeman. He stumbles upon an abandoned farm where the smell of ammonia leads him to a kind of deflated bag with a hole in its side. The author tells us that it was actually an environmental suit for a creature which breathes ammonia. He also finds a piece of metal resembling a large pot, which he decides to wear as a kind of hat to keep his hands free, but the strap tightens around his head and he is unable to remove it. He heads for the nearby town, but every form of animal life including humans fall unconscious as he approaches. They recover, unharmed, once he has moved out of range again. For several days he wanders about while the army tries to pinpoint the source of the disturbance and bomb it. Eventually he manages to cut through the strap just as a bomb hits the crashed spaceship. No one but he will ever know the truth.

"Assignment on Pasik" (1949) is a standard other world adventure in which the protagonist crash lands on Pasik, a virtually unknown world. There he discovers that the natives – a kind of humanoid ant – have been essentially enslaved by a small group of human beings who live in a grotesque parody of high society. A local woman threatens to kill him but he disarms her and discovers that the Pasiki have been killed by the millions in order to bring about their complete subjugation. The planet is now a kind of retirement home for prominent human criminals. The protagonist uses an elaborate pretext to lure the crew of a supply ship away so that he and his companion can seize control and escape. The interaction between the two human characters is rather awkwardly described but the story itself is cleverly done.

"The Queen's Astrologer" (1949) takes place in an unspecified medieval style society. The use of ultrasonic sounds to affect people's emotional states is well advanced and the astrologer uses one such device to undermine his repressive queen and cause her death. "The Life Work of Professor Muntz" (1949) is a mildly humorous story about a man who invents a machine that can affect the borders between parallel time lines.

Jimmy Briggs is about to set off on an interstellar voyage in "The Lost Race" (1949) when he discovers that Danton, a man he knows has been abusive toward his wife, is a member of the crew. Danton's former romantic rival, Howell, is also aboard. Their ship is fueled by a substance so valuable that even tiny amounts can make people rich. Nevertheless, voyages between the stars involve months of boredom. Hovering in the background is the mystery of the Lost Race, a space traveling civilization that disappeared, and in the process made an apparently concerted attempt to destroy all traces of their existence.

Briggs and Howell find a surviving artifact of the Lost Race. It consists of a podium where memories and thoughts can be projected and viewed by an audience. At first they think that they are seeing reality, but in fact it is just manipulation of images in their brain. Danton, however, is vaguely precognitive and he sees his wife cheating on him. The next day, someone sabotages the ship's engines, steals the precious fuel, and removes one of the lifeboats. Howell correctly assumes that it was Danton and proves it to the rest of the crew. Howell has disabled the lifeboat, however, and Danton is killed. As a final twist, we discover that the Lost Race killed itself because it was mutating into another form – humans.

"Doomsday Deferred" (1949, aka "The Soldado Ant") is quite short. A naturalist in a remote part of Brazil finds a peasant who is desperate to buy cattle. He subsequently learns that army ants have a mass consciousness and have effectively made the man and his family their procurement agents. "Cure for a Ylith" (1949) portrays the downfall of a cruel dictator when he uses a machine that allows him to communicate with his own superego.

"The Other World" (1949) is a novella. Dick Blair is an archaeologist who brings a peculiar find back to the US. It is a piece of metal that rusted in the middle of a desert. The tomb where it was found bears peculiar hieroglyphs suggesting that the occupant, an avowed magician, had extraordinary powers and a surprising grasp of human anatomy. There are claims that he made people disappear in a burst of quicksilver, which is mirrored by scattered similar events in the contemporary world. Blair and Sam Todd are investigating a series of puzzling disappearances when Blair falls in love with Nancy Holt, their brainy assistant.

The artifact is restored and proves to be a hand mirror that provides access to some kind of parallel world. They have just made that discovery when Holt literally disappears. Further analysis fortunately leads to the discovery of a way to cross into the other world invented by a man named Maltby. Blair decides to rescue Holt, while Todd is to monitor his progress and provide help if necessary.

Blair speculates that the original discoverers of the secret took refuge there and have since evolved a decentralized society in which each household is a law unto itself, taking slaves and other items from our world as desired. His theory proves true as he enters that world and discovers that human overseers are holding slaves abducted from our world. They use intelligent creatures resembling wolves to manage the work force, two of whom Blair kills within minutes of arriving.

Todd experiments with the viewing device and discovers that it is visible in the other world. A portable gate is employed to capture him, but he escapes by entering a subway, since the others have no way to access the underground and pursue him. Todd and Blair attempt to leave messages for each other, but the wolflike creatures intercept both. Blair is able to capture two small galleys and liberate their slaves, but with only spears and Blair's own firearms they are seemingly unable to effectively resist when a much larger ship attacks, along with wolves from the shore. But Blair uses a tear gas bomb to disable the men aboard the larger galley and soon adds its crew to their growing force of rebels. Unfortunately, Maltby and all of his equipment have been taken to the other world.

Todd is in a panic until he receives a call from Holt, who has returned from the other world with an escaped slave named Kelly. Holt's perfume is the scent worn by the masters of the slave world, so the wolves deferred to her long enough for her to find Kelly, spray him as well, and then use one of the traps to escape back to our reality. Holt, Kelly, and Todd arm themselves and cross the barrier, but rather stupidly the two men forget to bring the scent with them. Holt however is better prepared.

Blair intercepts a messenger and learns the masters' plans. He is leading an attack on a slave pen when the other party arrives and the defenders are slaughtered. The story concludes with the opening successes of a wide scale rebellion which we can assume eventually wipes out all of the slaveholders. Although by tone this is science fiction, the mirror devices are arguably magical, which would make the story a fantasy.

"The Lonely Planet" (1949) is one covered by a single, shapeshifting amoebalike creature that responds to human thought. A mining operation is established with only six humans in its complement, while the organism – Alyx – does all of the physical work. But Alyx grows more intelligent and is recognized as potentially dangerous. Humans withdraw, hoping that automated operations will be sufficient, but Alyx will not work unless humans are on the planet. Rather than allow Alyx to read the minds of experts, the company sends a crew with low intelligence. That makes it necessary for Alyx to become inventive in order to satisfy their demands, one of which results in unexpected and unwelcome planetary seismic activity. The company also notices that Alyx has designed new machinery, which they take and sell off world, but that brings them to the attention of the Space Patrol, which seizes control of the planet on the basis that Alyx is being exploited.

Eventually it is decided that Alyx must be destroyed because it is smarter than humans, but the attack is not a success. Alyx fashions shields and other weaponry that successfully defend the planet. When the shields drop, Alyx is gone, taking the planet with it. Alyx reappears at various times, takes human prisoners for periods of time to assuage its feelings of loneliness. Ultimately, Alyx leaves the galaxy, finds an expedition trying to reach the next galaxy and provides them with a home as it engages in its own private voyage through the universe.

"Be Young Again!" (1950) is narrated by a young man in a future where life spans are extended tremendously and space travel is a reality. True immortality is still a dream but a new discovery may hold the secret of restoring youth. An unauthorized substitution of one ingredient has unexpected consequences. The story is told in present tense, a very unusual device for its time and an experiment Leinster would not repeat.

"Nobody Saw the Ship" (1950) introduces an alien secretly visiting Earth who is seeking a particular hormone which can apparently be harvested from animal brains. The alien explores his surroundings in a vehicle designed to simulate a mountain lion. A local shepherd and his dog come upon some of the animals killed by the alien, but not eaten of course, and immediately suspect something is wrong. The dog later tangles with the alien, which retreats to its ship, only to discover after takeoff that insects have gotten inside and that it is doomed. "This Star Shall Be Free" (1949) is a minor piece in which visiting aliens perform an experiment on primitive humans which will lead to humans evolving into a space traveling species.

"Planet of the Small Men" (1950) opens with an attack on a human starship by an alien vessel despite longstanding belief that no other race in the galaxy had progressed far enough to travel among the stars. Even worse, the attacker appears to have a more advanced technology. The humans try to crash their ship into the ocean of an unknown planet but their attacker uses a tractor beam to land them safely on the land. The four humans immediately head away from their ship, but for some reason it is subsequently destroyed by an atomic missile. This does not seem consistent with the aliens' efforts to prevent the ship from destroying itself, but an explanation is on its way.

Adding to the confusion is the presence of a third alien race, this one indigenous to the planet and with an apparently primitive technology. The author then provides some back story. Humans are descended from a great and now vanished interstellar civilization which was almost completely destroyed and which is believed to have found a way to see into the future. They may have seen that their race was mutating and subsequently committed mass suicide. Humans are descended from a few children who were spared. So too, we gather, are the inhabitants of this planet, who look like humans but are much smaller.

The natives are very welcoming and seem almost childlike, even though the hostile aliens have destroyed one of their cities. They have the technology to look back through time and space and are aware that an entire fleet of their attackers is en route. They also have broadcast power and this is what prevented the human ship from crashing. With remarkable speed, they construct a spaceship which easily destroys the attackers. Rather too easily, as a matter of fact, since there is absolutely no doubt about the outcome of the battle and therefore no real tension.

"Historical Note" (1951) is a mildly humorous story about how the invention of the personal flying machine leads to the collapse of the Soviet Union. The protagonist of "The Other Now" (1951) is recently bereaved on the night that he has to open his front door twice in order to enter his house. He begins to find evidence that his dead wife is still alive, including her diary entry that refers to his having died. He eventually finds a way to cross over to her timeline and they are reunited. An alternate protagonist is not mentioned.

"Skag with the Queer Head" (1951) deals with mutation. Professor Danil was dismissed from his position because of his dubious experimental methods and now lives in a remote part of Canada. His research involves mentally enhanced dogs, one of whom is named Skag. Although never specifically described, his theory involves retarding the changes normally expected in the shape of the head. He killed the first litter of puppies Skag fathered by experimenting on them and now the dog's mate, Deena, has produced a second litter. Danil attempts to take one of the puppies to his laboratory but the two adult dogs seize him by the wrists. A duel of wits ensues which ends with Danil freezing to death. This was another rare story with a villainous protagonist.

"If You Was a Moklin" (1951) is set on an inhabited world where humans have established a trading post. The Moklins are humanoid and, rather oddly, the more contact they have with humans the more closely they resemble them. In fact, some of those who work at the trading post could almost pass for individual humans who have worked there in the past. The Moklins can partially control their own evolution.

An inspector arrives, the first human woman on the planet, and she is arrogant, uninformed, and uncooperative. She assumes the human agents have been breeding with the natives. She is also upset that another trading post has been opened, offering knockoffs of their own stock at lower prices. No one has ever seen the actual staff, however, so no one knows who is responsible. Obviously the Moklins are learning to be human, literally evolving into a new race. When the human complement realizes this, they immediately evacuate the planet to prevent Moklins from entering human society at large. The narrator, however, turns out to be a Moklin and he plans to bring others off the planet.

There are living inhabitants on the Moon in "Keyhole" (1951). They do not need oxygen and thanks to the brutality of an early expedition, they are hostile to humans and attack them by throwing rocks that are sharp enough to pierce a spacesuit. Humans have decided to exterminate them and the protagonist is a scientist who is reluctantly experimenting with a captured alien child to learn more about them. Eventually he realizes that the aliens are telepathic, that they planted the child in order to learn how to defend themselves from humans. Fortunately they are willing to co-exist.

"Devil's Henchman" (1952) is a rare excursion into the supernatural involving a magic ring that shows people the person you really are. "The Barrier" (1952) is a rather dull story about a man who figures out how to turn ordinary equipment on a spaceship into a faster than light drive.

"The Gadget Had a Ghost" (1952) is a time travel story. An American academic in Turkey is confronted by a centuries old manuscript that bears his fingerprints and a cryptic message about a gadget and possibly the murder of his prospective father-in-law. The police are perplexed but interested. They cannot find the gadget where it is supposed to be located, but a portion of that room is inexplicably cold and wet. Attempts are made on the life of the man mentioned in the note, but it appears that the protagonist is not responsible for them. The cold spot is presumably the ghost of the gadget, which still exists only in the past. Eventually they conclude that the gadget is a communication device created by an alchemist, and that they need to complete the cycle in order to ensure that history does not change.

In "The Castaway" (1953) Ben Lyon spots a fireball coming to Earth somewhere near the small town where he lives. The next day he and some friends encounter a being that hides in the darkness and speaks in the voice of one of their group, indicating that it is a castaway and wants to make friends. There is disagreement about whether or not the castaway should be immediately killed to prevent contact with a much more advanced civilization. After two failed attempts to kill the alien, the authorities believe that it has taken the life of a human child and a general manhunt gets underway. But the child turns up unharmed. The alien visits Lyons, who tells him that it is regrettable but that he must be killed, so the alien fakes his own death. Only Lyons knows the truth, and realizes that the castaway will eventually seek knowledge of human nuclear science. The story is very well told, although the conclusion is rather depressing.

The protagonist of "Overdrive" (1953) is involved in the investigation of the murder of four planetary populations when the star liner he is traveling on has a malfunction of its overdrive, which is essentially a death sentence. A politician and his daughter tell him that they think the malfunction was the result of a plot to murder them for something they discovered while visiting a planetary dictator. He also discovers that the ship's bar is serving drinks laced with a substance that causes murderous rages and concludes that the crew is planning to kill the diplomat under the cover of a riot, after which the overdrive will be mysteriously repaired.

Our hero conveniently knows how to reconfigure the overdrive so that it is much faster, but so complex that the crew cannot understand it. Once it is running, the crew is panicky. He also confides to the politician that he knows that the tyrant whose planet they just left is part of a secret group that has somehow mastered matter transmission. They send their fleet to poison the atmosphere of a planet and then loot it after everyone has died. With the ship in their control, the agent and politician are able to warn the authorities about what is going on. This was not a very good story, primarily because the hero has so much amazing knowledge that he is never really in jeopardy, but some of its premises were refined and used more effectively in novels late in the author's career.

"The Journey" (1953) is a coming of age story about a young man who ships out on a voyage to Pluto. Uncharacteristically for both the author and the genre at the time, the story shuns melodrama in favor of realism. He meets a young woman who has never seen an open sky and on the voyage back to Earth they fall in love and decide to get married.

"The Invaders" (1953) is a short novel. Coburn is visiting a remote part of Greece when a unit of Bulgarian soldiers crosses the border to raid a nearby village. He flees and encounters Janice Aymes, an aid worker, and a journalist named Dillon. But by chance, he discovers that Dillon is actually an alien wearing a suit to make him look human. A short time later, the entire invading force falls unconscious. Dillon intervenes to prevent the local people from killing them where they lay, but Coburn confronts him and he admits that he is not a human being. He sends Coburn and Aymes to alert the authorities to the raid.

News of the incursion is suppressed, but Coburn discovers that his secretary has been replaced by an alien that could be her twin. She leaves when he confronts her and assures him that the secretary has not been harmed. He also finds the real Dillon, who was never anywhere near the site of the invasion. When he unmasks an alien at a military conference, his story is accepted but once again the alien escapes without hurting anyone. When the military tries to move Aymes and Coburn to a more secure location, a flying saucer appears, but is shot down.

Hundreds of people disappear suddenly when a simple test is found to prove whether they are human or alien. Coburn, however, is inexplicably imprisoned by the authorities on the assumption that he is collaborating with the aliens, despite strong evidence to the contrary. An alien ship appears to be attacking the US Navy fleet in Naples, but all they do is render unconscious the crew of a foreign freighter, which is discovered to have been carrying nuclear weapons from the communist nations in an attempt to destroy the fleet. Eventually negotiations prove that the aliens are hoping to make friends. The resolution is extremely weak and predictable.

This story repeats a recurring theme in Leinster's work – that humans would instinctively view aliens as monsters, even when there is no evidence of malevolent intent. He does not express overt approval of this stance, but suggests that it is a survival instinct, understandable and perhaps even desirable, if unfortunate. There is also a small plot glitch. Once Coburn has told his story to the authorities, there is no longer a valid reason for the aliens to have attempted to capture him.

"The Sentimentalists" (1953) involves a colony world where the company that dominates it is exploiting colonists to keep them essentially in permanent debt. The protagonist and his girlfriend are caught in this trap and are despondent, but unbeknownst to them, a pair of honeymooning aliens with a much more advanced technology is watching them from another planet in the system. The aliens stimulate the man's mind so that he develops a power system that requires no fuel. When his food storage system fails, he discovers that he knows how to build a matter duplicator. When the local sun begins to misbehave, he figures out how to screen the entire planet. The local company representative calls in thugs to secure the secrets of the inventions by force, and the aliens intervene for the last time, paralyzing the thugs.

"Dear Charles" (1953) is a humorous story about time travel. A man from our time writes a "story" about his adventures in the future, so that they will eventually be read by a remote descendant he meets during his trip there. "The Little Terror" (1953) is a tale of the enfant terrible. A man tells his six year old granddaughter that she can make things disappear using a magical word. He means it as a joke, but she discovers that it really works. She "disappears" a number of things before he convinces her that saying it backwards will bring them back, and also that the magic has all been used up and will not work any more.

"The Trans-Human" (1953) is about a human boy raised by a hostile alien race to believe that he is one of them. His mission to destroy Earth fails and he learns the truth. "The Psionic Mousetrap" (1955) is a rather minor story about a spy in Russia who is captured and uses a mentally triggered teleportation machine to escape.

"Second Landing" (1954) is set in a distant future where humans have discovered that there were two rival interplanetary civilizations that wiped each other out in the distant past. In one set of ruins, they find a locket containing a picture of an apparently human girl. They also discover that something has dug up the garbage pit of an earlier expedition, and only a few days before their own landing.

A booby trap sets off a nuclear explosion, but fortunately the wind is blowing away from the human encampment. They relocate to a cave that had once been a kind of bomb shelter. The protagonist takes a flier and goes exploring, but is attacked by a primitive rocket whose pilot is the woman whose face is in the locket he found. He returns to the expedition, but his efforts to avoid being tracked fail and a nuclear weapon explodes nearby, sealing them in the cave. They escape, disable one of the hostile airships, and make friends with its crew after demonstrating that they are not members of the extinct race. It is a fair story, but it is hard to believe that after eight thousand years, the surviving race would still be searching the other planet to kill theoretical survivors.

"Fugitive from Space" (1954) utilizes a theme sometimes found in movies. Burt and Norma see mysterious lights in the sky one evening. Burt is driving home when some kind of gigantic parachute falls on his car. He has a vague sense that something is inside his mind before he loses consciousness. He wakes up in bed with his eyes bandaged. Someone calling himself John Smith tells him to stay in bed until the doctor comes, but he recognizes Smith's voice as his own.

The alien admits that it is a fugitive hiding on Earth and that it is altering its body to resemble humans. The alien's pursuers might destroy the planet if they knew it survived, and it is carrying a midget atomic bomb to avoid capture. Burt arranges to meet the alien later in the day and then confides everything to Norma. The alien takes them both prisoner a short time later and expresses its opinion that they are no better than animals relative to his race. It has a weapon that can temporarily paralyze them, and which later allows him to explode a tank truck to demonstrate his powers.

Burt realizes that the alien is color blind when it makes him buy makeup to color its lips and teeth. Later, while robbing a bank, the alien is struck by a car and temporarily incapacitated. Burt grabs its weapon and he and Norma escape in a car. Although they drive for hours, the alien has stolen another vehicle and it knows how to anticipate any decision Burt makes because it has his memories. Burt asks Norma to make choices after he realizes this, while a general uproar about a maniac rises after it kills several motorists. Burt eventually convinces the FBI and helps trap and kill the creature, but the ending is rather rushed.

"Honeymoon on Dlecka" (1955) is another story of humans misunderstanding aliens. A rather conceited young couple decides to spend their honeymoon on a planet inhabited by an aboriginal species. They want to commemorate their love by "uplifting" the natives to a supposedly more desirable human form of civilization. The Dlecka are empaths and they are obsessed with being near the humans, except when the latter are angry. The woman teaches them sculpture which eventually results in some rather obscene portraits of the two humans, who eventually leave the planet. Years later, the obscene statues become something of a galactic sensation.

"Sam, This Is You" (1955) is a convoluted but very amusing story about a telephone repairman who gets a phone call from his future self. He is able to capture some bank robbers thanks to a tip from his alternate self. "White Spot" opens with four people crashing on an uninhabited planet where a white spot hundreds of miles in diameter forms into a mirror to try to destroy their ship with a beam of heat. They come to ground a fair distance away, hoping to repair their ship, and dealing with one of their number – Sattell – whom the others do not trust. They treat him as a virtual prisoner, but one day he disappears. There are primitive natives who appear friendly and eventually they find the ruins of a more technological civilization. The white spot turns out to be a giant intelligent kind of amoeba but they destroy it with microwaves.

"Scrimshaw" (1955) takes place in a mining colony on the dark side of the Moon. Pop Young lives alone in a tiny dome on the surface. The miners almost invariably develop agoraphobia during their time at the site and many have to be drugged in order to be evacuated. Young developed amnesia during an attack that killed his family, and one of the new miners, Sattell, looks familiar to him. He eventually sabotages a robot ship like the ones that take men away, and then lets Sattell know that his memories have come back and he has arranged it so that Sattell can never leave the mine.

"Women's Work" (1956) is another minor story about a missile defense post that is operated exclusively by women and the upset that occurs when an escaped male prisoner joins them. "The Machine That Saved the World" (1957) is an early story of artificial intelligence. Many machines have been fitted with AI compatibility but there are some troublesome, indecipherable broadcasts that interfere with communications. There is one maintenance machine nicknamed Betsy, the only machine not to break down and the only one to accurately record the message, and that attracts attention. Fragments are decoded and they include the assertion that the messages come from the future and are meant as a warning. Eventually the messages indicate that a plague is imminent, and that the people in the present should build a device that would allow them to communicate with the future and deal with it. It turns out to be a fraud perpetrated by communists.

"Anthropological Note" (1957) takes place on the now scientifically disproven jungle version of Venus. There are primitive humanoid inhabitants known as Krugs. The male Krugs gather ornate shells and pearls which are highly prized on Earth. Only females and children live in their villages and little is known about them. A woman named Cummings has come to Venus to find a way to acquire the shells and get rich. She is unaware that Ray Hale, a known criminal, is also on the planet.

Cummings sets out to learn the local language, plural actually since males and females use different vocabularies. She is particularly perplexed that neither has a term equivalent to "Why?" She continues to study them while Hale accumulates a fortune in pearls by killing male Krugs and stealing their property. Then a problem arises. The most senior matron notes that Cummings has no children and is too old, in their terms, to find a husband. She suggests that Cummings kill herself and the anthropologist finds herself ostracized by the rest of the community.

Cummings is subsequently surprised when she is chosen for the marriage ceremony. The Krugs have captured Hale and he is to be her mate. Cummings knows Hale personally and hates him passionately. She questions him and finally lets him go, but unbeknownst to either of them, Krug husbands are killed by the other females after they have mated and Hale is buried in a small garden.

"A Short History of World War Three" (1958) is a minor piece about the use of psionics to anticipate actions by the Soviet government. "A Matter of Importance" (1959) is rather too long for its content. A distress call leads the authorities to discover an outpost of an alien race who fought humans in the past, but now humans want them as allies.

"The Aliens" (1959) is still another first contact story. Humans know of the existence of another star travelling race, the Plumies, because they have found artifacts on uninhabited worlds, but they have never actually encountered the others and there is uncertainty about possible hostility. Jon Baird is a crewman on a ship that discovers a lone Plumie ship in an uncharted solar system. He is concerned because Taine - the tactical officer aboard - is a known xenophobe, part of a policy to place such people aboard in case of conflict that requires consideration of opposing points of view before making a decision..

The alien ship performs maneuvers that appear threatening and the humans fire missiles at it. The missiles are disabled by tractor beams from the aliens, but the two ships collide and their hulls are welded together. They are also falling into the sun. The human space drive is totally destroyed. The alien drive will not operate and only the humans realize that it is because of the magnetic field generated by their own ship. The two races exchange brief visits to each other's ship and both are aware that in less than two weeks they will be destroyed if they cannot find a solution. The humans finally decide to cut the Plumie ship free since it can function once it is away from their magnetic field, and the aliens respond by using their tractor beams to save the human ship.

Leinster frequently dealt with the difficulties of communicating with aliens, and this story provides a plausible scenario with the exception of Taine, who at one point tries to smuggle a bomb onto the other ship. The idea that a psychopath would knowingly be put in a critical situation involving first contact is not credible, particularly one who is insubordinate and marginally insane.

"Thing from the Sky" (1960) is an invasion story. An alien hopes to clandestinely plant seeds of a new weed which will overwhelm the Earth, but mischance leaves him stranded and ignorance thwarts the effort because the plants are unable to produce new seeds on Earth. The protagonist actually feels sympathy for the invader, who is accidentally stranded and commits suicide.

A spaceman hijacks a starship in "Rogue Star" (1960) to examine a nearby antimatter star, but he inadvertently takes two technicians along with him. He hopes to take advantage of the negative time flow to go back twenty years and become famous. But he misjudges the effect, ends up in prehistory, where he introduces agriculture to the hunter gatherer culture he finds there.

"Attention Saint Patrick" (1960) is a non-serious story about an Irish colonized planet that is plagued by miniature dinosaurs. "The Leader" (1960) is an epistolary story which explains that the immense popularity of a ruthless dictator was the result of his powers to affect the mind of people around him. "Tyrants Need to Be Loved" (1960) is somewhat similar except that in this case a planetary dictator is using psychological techniques to manipulate the loyalties of his subjects.

"The Ambulance Made Two Trips" (1960) features a police officer named Fitzgerald who has been receiving anonymous gifts that he believes come from a local crime boss. The same thing is happening to other members of the force and Fitzgerald believes that many of his fellow officers are finding themselves unwillingly predisposed to think less badly of the criminal, even if they are not consciously corrupt. He personally has been donating everything he receives to a local orphanage.

Fitzgerald is also curious about a man named Brink, who is at odds with the gang. Odd accidents have been happening to the men sent to intimidate him, however, and Fitzgerald notices that he has an interest in unusual mental powers. Brink, it turns out, has psionic devices which alter probability in his favor. He and Fitzgerald eventually use them to defeat the entire gang and send the leaders to jail.

"The Corianus Disaster" (1960) makes use of another familiar Leinster premise, the starship that disappears while en route from one world to another. The Corianus was carrying a number of political figures who were negotiating a trade treaty. They experience a very rare collision in space but are able to repair their drive and proceed. However, when they arrive at their destination, they find that an exact duplicate of the ship and its passengers has already landed, and they did not experience the collision. There are seven people on one ship who do not appear on the other, including Jack Bedell, the protagonist. Clearly the two ships are from slightly different realities. The local populace becomes very uneasy and riots ensue until Bedell convinces them to reverse course, duplicate their unfortunate encounter, and return to their own universe.

"Doctor" (1961) involves a deadly new virus that threatens to exterminate all life on human occupied worlds. A doctor discovers that a passenger aboard his ship has been exposed, but he is able to find a way to treat it before it spreads. "The Case of the Homicidal Robots" (1961) is another space opera. Various ships have disappeared in space but since it is believed to be impossible to find anything in hyperspace, no one suspects piracy. Kilmer was aboard one of the missing ships, and survived because he was in a lifeboat when the ship began acting strangely and ejected him. No one believes his story, however. Kilmer begins studying robots, who supposedly cannot injure humans, and then hears of an incident where a robot ship that was being dismantled killed several human workers. He is in the process of delivering a privately built ship when it begins to act strangely. He disables the various things that could be turned to lethal use and theorizes that humans are altering the robots at the spaceport where the ship took off so that they can no longer recognize the presence of humans. This allows the ships to be diverted by pirates, or actually a single piratical mastermind who also proves to be quite insane. Kilmer outwits and kills him.

"Planet of Dread" (1962) is a sequel to *The Forgotten Planet*. Moran is a fugitive who is about to be marooned on an uncharted planet because his presence when they next land will raise too many questions about an extra passenger. Somewhere on the planet a crashed spaceship is still emitting a weak distress signal. The humans encounter warring ant cities, a twenty foot tall praying mantis, and other monstrosities, while discovering that the crashed ship has valuable minerals aboard. One of the other men plots to kill his shipmates and keep the fortune for himself, but his intentions are discovered and killed, which makes it possible for Moran to take his place.

The laws of nature are temporarily suspended in "Imbalance" (1962) and a man on the brink of bankruptcy has an incredible run of luck at the Las Vegas casinos. A space explorer finds the ruins of an alien civilization and a secret that he uses to end the aggressive actions of the communist world back on Earth in "The Third Planet" (1963). "Manners and Customs of the Thrid" (1963) is a nicely told story about a man's experiences on a planet where the local rulers are by definition never wrong. "A Planet Like Heaven" (1966) takes place on a planet where carnivorous trees are harvested by imported and reasonably intelligent elephants, who are effectively enslaved by human traders. When the company introduces draconian measures to increase production, they precipitate a rebellion and are driven off the planet.

When NESFA Press released its retrospective collection of Leinter's short fiction, *First Contacts* (1998), they included two previously unpublished stories. "The Great Catastrophe" was written in 1919 and sold to a magazine which died before publishing it. The story is of historical interest only, describing the Earth after a catastrophic collision with an object from space. "To All Fat Policemen" is a non-fantastic vignette about immigrants.

The Med Service Series

Leinster rarely wrote sequels or series characters, the most noteworthy exception being the stories and short novels about Dr. Calhoun, who travels interstellar space dispensing medicine. Calhoun first appeared in "Ribbon in the Sky" (1957). Calhoun is a doctor who patrols his assigned sector of the galaxy alone except for the presence of Murgatroyd, a tormal, an alien monkeylike creature whose body has the ability to create antibodies to almost any disease, which makes him an excellent diagnostic tool and the key to treating unknown new plagues. His ship is the Aesclipus Twenty.

His ship emerges from overdrive in an unknown region of space, thanks to some malfunction. He finds a barely habitable planet nearby whose inhabitants have created a ribbonlike band of particles to reflect more sunlight down to the surface. The planet has a landing grid and they bring him down, but they are hostile and refuse to allow him to leave his ship.

It appears that there are only three cities, each hostile to the other two, and that the planet has been isolated from outside contact for a long time. He is presently in City One, but a handful of people from City Two visit clandestinely and spirit him off to their community. They appear to be afraid of catching something from him and all of them wear masks.

It appears that each city believes that the other two harbor some fatal disease, so when two sentries meet and become romantically involved, they are quarantined and sentenced to death. The young woman's father, Hunt, offers to exile himself as penance when the two run away, but he is convinced they will also die of exposure. Calhoun suggests that the two of them find the runaways and try to learn the truth about the possibility of contagion.

Calhoun suspects that the three cities have been isolated from each other long enough for them to lose their immunities to diseases from the other communities. He and Hunt take the runaways to a more habitable part of the planet, and he notes that none of the three local people has become ill. The old illnesses have all died off, so he tricks the population into thinking that they have been cured.

The Mutant Weapon (1957, aka *Med Service*), a novella,

followed shortly thereafter. The series includes a second novella, This *World Is Taboo*, and several short stories which were collected as *Doctor to the Stars* and *S.O.S. from Three Worlds*. An omnibus edition appeared in 2002 as *Med Ship*.

Calhoun's current mission is to the newly colonized world Maris III for what should have been a routine visit. When he requests that the colony use their landing grid to bring his ship to the planet's surface, he is almost killed when his ship is hurled wildly about by the grid's force beams. He manages to break free with some difficulty and lands using his own rockets.

Calhoun does some reconnaissance. The city appears to be deserted and there is no radio traffic, but he spots another ship that appears to be searching for him. He sets off on foot toward the city and the following day finds a man who apparently starved to death even though he is lying in a field of edible crops. Murgatroyd is able to eat the crops, so there is no possibility of poison.

A young woman named Helen Jons attempts to kill Calhoun with a crossbow. She shows signs of malnutrition and a blood sample suggests oxygen deprivation. Jons describes a sudden plague that left its victims so weak they could not eat. The first full shipload of colonists was told not to land and they left the system, but they were followed by another ship with unknown occupants who began killing anyone who still survived.

Calhoun uses the blood sample to infect Murgatroyd, who displays symptoms very quickly. They travel to the girl's camp where they find some of her fellow survivors have been recently murdered. Calhoun sets up an ambush, assuming the killer will return for the others. He does so but Calhoun is forced to kill him with the crossbow and cannot interrogate him. It is obvious now that the newcomers are using the plague to depopulate the colony so that they can loot it.

Using Murgatroyd's antibodies, Calhoun treats the remaining survivors. He believes that the invaders planned this outcome from the outset and that there are shiploads of colonists en route from another planet to steal the colony. He is also convinced that the creator of the new plague – which results from the juxtaposition of two separately inoffensive elements – is in the city directing the operation.

Calhoun sneaks into the city and uses a long lasting anesthetic spray to knock out a few of the invaders, simulating an attack of plague. He gains access to the invaders' ship and incapacitates the man running the operation. Then he leaves, setting up a deadfall that kills at least one of the others, then steals a vehicle and heads away from the city with some of the others in hot pursuit. He later manages to ambush and disable them all by luring them into a building he has rigged with the knockout gas.

The survivors show up and Calhoun has them communicate with the ship full of illegal colonists who are now in orbit and claim that the original plague mutated and that virtually everyone is dead. This causes them to head back home as well as undercutting their confidence that the new plague would allow them to take over multiple planets similarly. The man responsible for the plague is left to the mercy of his former subordinates.

"The Grandfather's War" (1957) assumes that interplanetary warfare is virtually impossible since landing grids are the only way to land or take off – this is not actually true since rocket powered ships have to land the people to build them. Calhoun has been requested to visit a system about to engage in a war to deal with casualties, which he considers a waste of time since he does not expect there to be any. When he arrives, his ship is disabled and he discovers that someone has indeed found a way to wage war in space. It consists of constructing a landing grid which is itself a spaceship.

The inhabitants of one of the opposing worlds believed that their sun is about to nova, so they sent their younger generation to another system to build a new colony. The younger people, however, are convinced that it was just a hoax to get them to build the colony and they refuse to allow their elders to relocate. Calhoun finds that their social relations are not interacting properly, that the youngest are in rebellion against the older ones, that infighting and petty rivalries are causing disruptions, and that there is an over reliance on virtual reality to take care of the youngest children.

Calhoun orders the planet quarantined as a disease ridden slum. The young people refuse to believe him, of course, but a general epidemic conveniently breaks out the next day. Calhoun finds a cure for the disease, destroys an incoming missile, and talks them out of fighting a war. The point is supposedly that a society cannot function unless all age levels are present.

This was not one of Leinster's more logical stories. The characterization of the two societies is overly simplified and implausible. The conflict is terribly contrived. The irresponsibility of the entire younger culture is disturbingly stereotyped and the examples we see are caricatures rather than realistically drawn people.

This World Is Taboo (1961, aka *Pariah Planet*) was the second novella. Calhoun is to make a long overdue general inspection of Weald Three. The local authorities are initially reluctant to let him land and then seem inordinately worried that he might be a "blueskin," the term for a condition in which survivors of a particular plague retain blue pigment in their skin. It is peculiar to another planet - Dara.

After landing, Calhoun finds no evidence that there have ever been any blueskins on the planet. A local doctor tells him that it is a political device used to influence the voters and keep them in a constant state of simmering fear. Children are taught that the blueskins are plague carriers and spread the contagion deliberately. Weald maintains a blockade of Dara, which is in desperate need of food, depriving it of the vast surplus of grain from Weald, more than enough to feed everyone. They also have a small mining colony on a planet halfway between the two systems.

There is an uproar when a mysterious ship enters the system but refrains from communicating or approaching the planet. It is from Orede, the mining planet, and has almost the entire colony aboard, all long since dead from lack of sufficient air. The political leaders immediately blame Dara and begin preparations for a genocidal bombing from space. Disgusted, Calhoun sets out for Orede, and soon discovers that a young girl has stowed away. She refuses to tell him the real reasons motivating her.

Calhoun correctly guesses that she is a Darian spy and that others from her planet went to Orede because it has a large population of cattle. They arrive at the colony and find most of it wrecked, apparently by stampeding cattle. Calhoun is not able to raise anyone on the radio and while he is trying to do so, the woman – Maril - sneaks out of the ship to go look for her countrymen. Calhoun follows and just barely saves her from another stampede.

They are attacked by Darians on their way back to the ship. Calhoun broadcasts a warning telling them to evacuate before they are found, then takes off for Dara. Maril confirms that there is a planetwide famine and that is why they were harvesting cattle on Orede. When they reach Dara, Calhoun becomes a virtual prisoner as they plan to use his ship to spread a plague on Weald. Calhoun quietly destroys the plague virus en route while training his guards, all conveniently space pilots, how to improve their skills. They seize four of the unmanned grain ships that Weald has conveniently placed in orbit to hold excess crops.

Calhoun's ship is the first to return to Dara, where his story is doubted and he is sentenced to death despite Maril's confirmation. This part of the plot is not particularly realistic, and in any case one of the grain ships arrives just in time to prevent his execution. He has also been carefully creating another virus that will eliminate the retention of blue pigment, thereby eliminating blue skins.

Weald sends a war fleet to Dara. They are told that the captured ships have been fitted with fusion bombs and sent to Weald. If Dara is attacked, so also will Weald. The Darians also offer to pay for the stolen grain with heavy metals not found in quantity on Weald. The Darians offer to allow the ships from Weald to land and to let their crews, safely wearing suits impervious to contagion, loot their cities. After a few days of this, each Wealdian ship has Darians aboard – apparently they have very lax security – who seize control of the ships and force the commander to sue for peace.

The story is an obvious commentary on the irrationality of racism and the amorality of politics. Unfortunately, the author suggests removing the difference rather than educating the populace to remove bigotry. In the real world, they would just have found some other reason to oppress an outside group.

The resolution depends on a completely untenable premise. Why would the planet Weald store all of its excess grain in orbit? What would be the point of the unnecessary expense? There is also some patronizing chauvinism. When Maril opines that she would like to have piloted one of the grain ships, Calhoun dismisses her sentiments. "You wouldn't want to be a heroine. No normal girl does."

"Tallien Three" (1963, aka "The Hate Disease") describes another routine inspection gone wrong. Tallien Three, which has not been inspected recently, is a jungle world whose ecology is so difficult to manage that only one of several continents has ever been colonized. Upon arriving in orbit, Calhoun receives conflicting signals from two different sources. Rockets are fired at his ship during landing, and an assassination attempt is barely foiled when he steps out.

The local government tells Calhoun that the enemy are the paras, victims of a contagion which they compares to demonic possession. The paras – short for paranoid – are already nearly a third of the population. Symptoms are a craving for an unusual food – a kind of parasite introduced as a scavenger - and hostility toward normals. The authorities suspect that it might be the result of exposure to some unknown life form native to the planet.

Calhoun realizes that the government officials are also secretly paras and manages to escape. Dr. Lett, the chief medical officer, seizes power and insists that he has found a cure. He has not, but Calhoun does. Since fires are rare on the planet, a component found in wood smoke has been missing from the atmosphere. So he starts a major fire in order to bring about a cure.

"Med Ship Man" (1963) takes Calhoun to a planet outside his usual patrol area. Maya seems perfectly ordinary from space, but when he arrives, there is no response to his radio call and another ship in orbit reports the same lack of communication. The second ship carries a passenger who insists upon being landed but Calhoun puts that issue on hold while he makes an emergency descent on rocket power. Even before he has landed, he notes that there is no sign of life in the nearby city.

All of the ground vehicles in the city are missing, suggesting an evacuation. Much of the plant life appears to have died and is decaying. There is no sign of the usual chaos of an evacuation, suggesting that it was planned in advance. Calhoun locates a ground car, determined to find out where the evacuees went, but before he can do so the indignant passenger descends from orbit via a small emergency pod and Calhoun feels obliged to make sure he is all right.

The stranger is Arthur Allison, an unpleasant man who insists he has important business on Maya. Murgatroyd has some unexplained muscle spasms. Calhoun becomes suspicious of Allison and asks questions about his background, which provokes Allison to attempt to draw a weapon. Calhoun knocks him out before he can do so. Then Calhoun feels the effects of an invisible force field designed to make him uneasy. He concludes that Allison had one deployed to drive the residents out of their city and lower their property values so that he could buy real estate. Calhoun leads a team to disable the device and the population returns to the city.

"Plague on Kryder II" (1964) changes the formula very slightly. This time the planet in question has sent a distress call, so Calhoun is prepared for trouble before he arrives. This particular plague consists of a cascade of diseases. Victims become progressively weaker and unable to resist the new ailments. Similar plagues have been reported on two other planets. On one of these, a tormal died of infection, which was theoretically impossible, and in the other, the med ship and its doctor were killed in an unexplained accident.

Calhoun makes the three week jump but when he emerges from hyperspace, all of the instruments in his ship insist that he is still on the ground at headquarters. He proceeds cautiously and discovers that despite the illusions, the ship is actually in empty space. When he cycles the airlock, the ship spontaneously sends an unknown message. Clearly someone has tried to kill him. He hides when two men come aboard the ship and disable the equipment which overrode the normal readings.

One of the men leaves and the other takes over the ship and heads for the plague planet. Calhoun captures him and lands on an uninhabited world, threatening to leave the man there unless he explains how he and his cronies were introducing the plague to colony worlds. Unfortunately he miscalculates and is forced to kill the man without learning anything.

He is supposed to work with a Dr. Kelo on Kryder II, but Calhoun suspects, correctly, that the man is working with the criminals. This is confirmed when he subdues the man operating the landing grid and tries to crash the med ship. He manages to land manually and clandestinely takes samples of all imported foodstuffs from a store. He discovers a substance which inhibits the formation of antibodies, which is why people are hit with a succession of diseases they could ordinarily resist. But the substance actually makes Murgatroyd sick, which is unheard of.

Calhoun returns to space, cures Murgatroyd, and radios the solution to the authorities. Kelo and his associates have become fugitives. They flee into space but Calhoun out maneuvers them and disables their ship, which crashes with no survivors.

"Quarantine World" (1966) was the final Med Service story. Calhoun is checking up on the planet Lanke, where the public health system seems too good to be true, which makes him suspicious. There is a violent disturbance while he is meeting with the local health officials, and although they minimize it, he believes they are hiding something. A quick examination of the body of a man killed during the incident turns up old scar tissue and dental problems, both of which are unheard of with modern medical techniques. Clearly he is being lied to.

Calhoun manages to take a sample of blood stained cloth, from which he determines that the man is not a native of Lanke, and that he was infected with a virulent virus. The authorities immediately expel Calhoun from the planet, but he declares the world quarantined. Calhoun develops the plague virus but Murgatroyd, though he is sick, does not develop antibodies, so he cannot cure himself.

Then a bizarre event takes place in hyperspace. Somehow his and another ship have come into proximity, which is not supposed to be possible. The other ship is strangely configured but has a human crew. Calhoun helps it to redirect itself to an inhabited planet for repairs, but it fires a missile at him while departing. He avoids the missile and lands on the supposedly uninhabited world of Delhi, hoping to give Murgatroyd a chance to survive.

Mysteriously, Calhoun begins to recover once they have landed. Calhoun discovers that the planet is not devoid of humans after all when two local people board his ship and barricade it against literally hundreds of others. His new guests explain that anyone who leaves the planet develops the plague and acts as a carrier, but that it is dormant on Delhi itself. Lanke knew about it because they had an outbreak, but they suppressed that information for business reasons. They have been exiling undesirables to Delhi secretly ever since. After some mild complications, Calhoun finds a cure and is eventually able to leave Delhi and report the situation to the Med Service.

Leinster never wrote a blockbuster novel that would become the linchpin of his career. Instead he wrote a steady stream of mostly well written stories, some of which were remarkably inventive. He would probably have described himself as a craftsman rather than an artist. While much of his work – particularly outside of science fiction – has largely fallen into obscurity, he is likely to be remembered as one of the most consistently reliable of the genre's early writers, and the best of his work will almost certainly be read for many generations to come.

ALGIS BUDRYS

Algirdas Jonas Budrys (1931-2008), born in Prussia, was the son of a member of the Lithuanian government in exile during World War II and his family remained in the US following the Russian occupation. He sold his first science fiction story in 1952 and wrote dozens of short stories as Algis Budrys and under several pseudonyms. His fiction output declined after 1960 and he became better known as a reviewer and critic for the SF magazines. He also worked with the Writers of the Future contest and anthology series and edited a short lived magazine called *Tomorrow*.

Novels

Budrys' first published novel was *False Night* (1954) which he revised and expanded in 1961 as *Some Will Not Die*. Both books are expansions of the short story "Ironclad." The original novel opens with Matt Garvin wakening in a taxi in the ruins of New York City following a devastating plague which has destroyed civilization and killed most of the population. The rewrite adds a prologue which occurs several years later in which Joe Custis commands an armored car scouting a part of the supposedly reclaimed country that is populated largely by outlaws. He has a political officer with him who is interested in finding a man named Berendtsen, rumored to be alive although most people believe he was killed decades earlier. Berendtsen organized the Second American Republic, which comprised the Northeast and part of Canada and lasted ten years. Custis serves under the Seventh Republic.

Both stories then follow the same course. Garvin is alone when he runs into Margaret Cottrell, a young woman who is foolishly naïve as she attempts to take medicine from a drug store to help her father, who has been shot in the chest. Garvin helps her and both are nearly killed by a hidden sniper. The rewrite adds a substantial section about Garvin's earlier adventures, his recovery from the plague to find that the city is mostly empty and that the other survivors have largely descended into paranoia. He successfully finds a friend, Larry Ruark, who also survived, but Ruark has resorted to murder and cannibalism and Garvin quickly leaves him.

The original story jumps forward several months. Cottrell's father has died of his injuries and Garvin has taken his place. He has become ruthless in his search for supplies and is ready to kill others without warning. There is a three year jump after which Garvin kills a man who enters their apartment, but this leads to an introduction to their neighbors, Gustav Berendtsen and his wife Carol.

Over the course of the next few years, they add more families to their growing community. A rival organization springs up nearby and has to be destroyed. Berendtsen dies, but his son follows in his footsteps and eventually all of Manhattan is united. The expanded version adds considerable detail to this chain of events. The consolidation continues and even before Garvin dies, there is a growing rivalry between his son and Theodore Berendtsen. There are brief diversions to continue the story of Custis in the future.

While Berendtsen is off with the army, the Garvins effectively stage a coup. The army returns after winning all of its battles, but the atmosphere in New York has changed while they were gone. The government is now essentially a dictatorship and Berendtsen is declared a traitor. More time passes. Berendtsen is believed to have been killed by a mob. Robert Garvin dies in a duel. The political situation continues to deteriorate, evolving into a society with duels and family feuds. Budrys used the story to argue both sides of the argument about the need for unification and order as opposed to the supposed rights of individuals.

His second novel was *Man of Earth* (1958, expanded from *The Man from Earth*). Allen Sibley is a timid businessman in 2197, a future in which technology has led to stagnation. There are small colonies on Pluto and Venus but they are essentially failures. Sibley is startled one day when a stranger approaches him at his club and indicates that he knows of some of Sibley's illegal business practices. The man subtly suggests that his company's services may be needed if the truth is ever revealed.

Several years later, a partner in his hidden scheme dies suddenly and his personal papers are to be examined. Sibley knows this will certainly lead to his exposure so – desperate for a way out - he visits the company's offices. They admit that they cannot stop the inevitable investigation and suggest instead that he submit to a process that will quite literally alter his body beyond recognition, probably changing his personality as well.

Budrys is vague about the nature of the operation, but after a few hours Sibley is much more physically fit and looks younger than his years. His personality has already grown more assertive and he chooses John L. Sullivan as his new name. That evening he is drugged and put aboard a ship for the Pluto colony with virtually no money and no way of returning. En route he learns that there are about fifty thousand people on Pluto, with a few immigrants from Venus still arriving, but that the corporation that founded the colony is bankrupt so everyone is essentially marooned there.

With no visible means of support, Sullivan finds himself immediately enlisted in the army. He is faced with a hazing and does not know how to defend himself, but he is in better physical shape than most of the others and seriously injures two men. Now respected, he immediately picks up a sycophant named Liencer. The military training is brutal and there are regular fatalities. Sullivan wonders who they are training to fight, but it is clear from context that their perceived enemy is Earth.

A lengthy training sequence follows during which Liencer is clearly revealed to be using Sullivan to intimidate the other soldiers, although Sullivan does not cooperate when he realizes what is happening. His new personality is surprisingly naïve. He becomes cordially hated and feared by everyone else until the sergeant in charge has a long talk with him. Sullivan tells Liencer off publicly, but that fails to redeem him in the eyes of the others.

Sullivan makes friends with a woman who works at a restaurant off post. He begins to think of marriage and civilian life, but the military training is ratcheted up and it looks like war is imminent. But then representatives of the company that brought Sullivan there arrive and explain that this was all part of their plan to create a disciplined and aggressive body of people with which to colonize the stars, and eventually Sullivan accepts that they are right.

The novel is rather dated scientifically. Even with an artificial sun it is hard to believe that Pluto could be habitable enough that people could walk around outside without special equipment. The climax is ineffective and unconvincing, and suggests a rather depressing worldview. It is never understood why anyone would bother to train colonists when there is as yet no method of reaching other star systems in the first place.

Budrys' next novel was *Who?* (1958), which was made into a fairly loyal but rather uninteresting movie which unfortunately reveals the solution much too early. It was developed from a short story of the same title published in 1955 and has been unavailable for most of the time since its original publication.

Lucas Martino is a brilliant physicist whose laboratory was close to the Soviet zone in Germany when an explosion destroyed the building. He was taken by the Soviets to a hospital and held for four months, but is now being returned to the Allied zone, where he is met by Shawn Rogers, who works in security. But during his stay, much of Martino's body was replaced by metal including the installation of a shell around his head, and since the novel was written in the days before DNA identification was possible, there is literally no way to determine if he is an imposter, a brainwashed version of himself, or the altered but genuine Lucas Martino. The shell cannot be removed without killing him.

The main story alternates between efforts to identify him and flashbacks to Martino's youth, which do not help the reader decide his present authenticity. When Rogers and his staff are unable to come to a determination, Martino is removed from all sensitive work, pensioned off, and his last project is abandoned. Rogers, quietly demoted for his failure despite its impossibility, is assigned to follow up until the truth can be determined.

As a young man, Martino worked in a coffee shop for a year in order to raise enough money to attend a state college, planning to achieve grades high enough that he would be admitted to MIT. He is awkward about the opposite sex and has a chaste relationship for some years with a young woman named Edith, which ends when she marries someone else.

Martino – fake or real - impulsively goes to visit Edith, who is now a widow, but he bolts when her young daughter is frightened by his appearance. He runs across the city in a panic, faster than human because of his augmentations, and the men following him fear that he will overstress his body and die. Instead, one of them is killed in an automobile accident.

While under this stress, he briefly addresses a woman in Italian, which suggests that he really is Martino. A report arrives that Martino's college roommate, Francis Heywood, was actually a Soviet spy, and that he was reportedly killed in a suspicious airplane crash shortly after Martino was seized by the Soviets. His body was never found. Heywood was about Martino's size and would have been excellently placed to learn what he needed to know to impersonate Martino. Another flashback provides a glimpse of their friendship.

Martino visits an old professor, who is not cordial and who later admits he cannot say if it was Martino. The older Martinos have died and left their son the farm and he goes there and begins the painstaking job of restoring the house and clearing the land. Five years pass. Rogers is sent to the farm to offer Martino a job working on his old project, which has still not been completed. He turns the offer down. Rogers cannot resist asking him point black if he is Martino, and the man says "No."

The story ends with a flashback. The Soviets did indeed plan to turn Heywood into a duplicate and send him back instead, but the agent who set the bomb on the airplane was unhappy about the situation and altered the timer. Heywood died in the crash rather than escaping by parachute. The intelligence officer in charge of the operation has himself become strangely disturbed by his conversations with a man of metal and even considers the possibility that this was all a plan to preoccupy him and cause him to neglect his other duties. It was in fact the real Martino who was returned.

It is a shame that this novel has become so dated both scientifically and politically because it is extremely well written, far superior to his earlier novels. The characters are fully drawn, the puzzle is interesting, and the prose – particularly in the flashback sequences – is superb.

The Falling Torch (1959) includes a disclaimer that the invaders in the book have "no counterpart in human history," but given that Budrys' father was part of the Lithuanian government in exile following the Soviet occupation, that is probably not the case. The novel is expanded from a shorter version and incorporates "Hot Potato" and "The Man Who Did Not Fit."

The story opens in 2513 with the funeral of Michael Wireman. Geneva is the capital of the solar system, which includes three inhabited worlds, and which has recently been liberated from twenty-five years of domination by the Invaders, an achievement for which Wireman is considered responsible. The story then jumps back more than fifty years to a human colony at Alpha Centauri.

ARCHITECTS OF TOMORROW

Ralph Wireman, Michael's father, is the president of the human government in exile. Centaurus was Earth's only colony and it has grown much more powerful and influential than the home world, but had not intervened when the Invaders took control of Earth. He and the other exiles have grown old and many of them look upon their continuing meetings as futile. They have become more concerned with making new lives for themselves among the Centaurians than in returning to Earth and expelling the invaders.

Wireman has recently been told of a large stock of weapons that could be transferred to the resistance on speculation, to be paid for if the Invaders are defeated. His cabinet members point out that these are not enough to make a prolonged difference because the Invaders would simply bring back their military units, which would still be far superior in numbers and fire power. But Wireman believes that the arms are a ruse, a way that the Centaurian government can begin to assist them without being overtly involved, and he does not want the chance to slip aweay. A majority of the cabinet, however, have made new lives for themselves and do not want to drop everything now. Wireman calls for their resignations and they comply.

In a decision made off stage, Michael Wireman is chosen to be the focus of a rebellion. He secretly returns to Earth accompanied by Isaac Potter, a Centaurian, and a consignment of small arms. They make contact with the self-styled General Hammil, who seems to lead the only significant resistance movement. Wireman takes an immediate dislike to Hammil, considering him unfit to lead the rebels, but he is in no position to do anything about it.

Wireman soon learns that Hammil's lieutenants despise their commander as well and that he is stupid and cowardly, but Potter – who is an agent of military intelligence on Centaurus – tells him that they will force Hammil to fight the Invaders. He does in fact attack a command post, but only because he has a personal grudge against its commanding officer. The Invaders are essentially humans and their administration is not particularly repressive so there is not a great deal of popular support.

Potter is fatally wounded and admits to Wireman that his government has signed an agreement recognizing Hammil as president of Earth because it wants a weak man in that position. Disgusted, Wireman surrenders to the Invaders, who treat him surprisingly well, and he discovers that Hammil and the other holdouts are largely despised by the populace.

He does not find contentment with the Invaders either. His personality profile does not fit into their computerized system of vocations. The human psychologist in charge of his case, who never considered rebellion, finds his own attitude changing after they meet and he helps Wireman to escape. A guard is killed in the process and he takes shelter with an older woman who runs a shop. She also thought of herself as loyal to the Invaders, but the romantic image of helping a rebel is too appealing.

They concoct an elaborate plan to leave the city which presumably works out, although we do not see it in action. In fact, the story jumps right over the rebellion to a point sometime in the future. The Invaders have been driven off Earth and a Centaurian fleet is in the system, carrying Ralph Wireman and the other surviving cabinet members. Hammil is out of the picture. The elder Wireman considers himself leader of Earth but is quickly disabused of that notion. Michael, though not enthusiastic, has discovered that people get trapped into roles they feel they should play and do not realize that they are not free to change them. He also outmaneuvers the Centaurians, who want Earth to be a vassal state, insisting that the planet be fully independent.

Despite the melodramatic plot, this is a thoughtful and intellectual story that is primarily about the conflict within the minds of humans rather than the outward conflict of war. Many readers will be disappointed that the liberation is barely mentioned and in fact Michael never even demonstrates any leadership potential. We are only told retroactively of his accomplishments.

Rogue Moon (1960, aka *The Death Machine*) is a genre classic. Edward Hawks is in charge of a project to explore an alien artifact found on the moon. It is a large maze which kills whoever enters unless they somehow manage to adhere to a set of unknown and apparently arbitrary rules. Hawks has developed a kind of matter transmitter and duplicator that sends copies of men to the moon where they invariably die while exploring the structure. The stress of multiple deaths inevitably drives them mad because they have all those memories when they are recreated back on Earth.

Hawks decides that the solution is to find a man who is perhaps already unbalanced and who will be able to handle the experience of dying over and over again. A personnel manager named Connington leads him to recruit Al Barker, who has a death wish and a strong personality. Barker lives atop a cliff with a dangerous approach road, currently cohabiting with Claire Pack, his lover. Barker has an artificial leg and a record of taking wild chances, and almost always succeeding.

There is a four way psychological power play among the four named characters that is much more subtle and complex than is usually found in science fiction from the early 1960s. The initial meeting is confrontational and ends with Hawks walking down from the cliff and catching a ride with Elizabeth Cummings who stops for gas. There is an immediate attraction between them.

Barker shows up at the project, though he remains prickly. There is an exchange of quotes which introduces an Arthurian theme – Barker as Lancelot and Hawks as Merlin. Hawks' second in command dislikes Barker openly and Hawks has him replaced immediately. He needs fast results to avoid being shut down by either the company or the government and friendship has to take second place.

The preliminary scanning and tests are successful. Barker's duplicate is sent to the moon where he slightly extends the length of time a human has been able to stay alive inside the artifact, still less than four minutes. He is badly shaken when restored to consciousness on Earth, but is not insane.

Pack attempts to seduce Hawks but fails because she does not understand his nature. Barker, seeking a target for his anger, attacks Connington physically, and is stunned when Pack shows genuine affection for the injured man, which leads to the end of their own relationship. Barker considers withdrawing from the program, but after the confrontation with Pack, he reconsiders.

Barker tells Hawks that he believes he will reach the exit on his next visit. Hawks surprises everyone by announcing that he will be accompanying Barker this time. They are successful but it is only then that Hawks explains to Barker that there is no way to return to Earth because they do not have a reliable transmitter on the moon. And even if they did, there would be two identical versions of themselves already established there. Hawks decides to wait for his air to run out but Barker goes to one of the domes instead, planning to wait until he can be transported back. So it is Hawks rather than Barker who ultimately embraces death.

Although this is science fiction, it could easily have been mainstream fiction. The story is not about the artifact on the moon but is rather about the personalities and interactions of the four main characters, each of whom is starkly drawn. Hawks describes himself as a murderer but asserts that he has no choice. Barker considers himself a warrior, but Hawks points out that he is more afraid of appearing weak or frightened than of actually dying. Pack is somewhat honest in that she admits that she deliberately provokes men but even that admission is part of her strategy. Connington is a schemer who does not understand that the rules are even more complex than he imagined.

The novel includes brief discussions of what it means to be a man, or a woman, of the role of intelligence in human civilization, of the nature of romance and friendship, and of the obligations we have to one another. There are multiple duels other than the competition with the enigmatic device on the moon – and none of Barker's encounters there occur on stage until the very last one. We only get brief reports later. Each of the characters is consciously attempting to manipulate the others. It is a tour de force of character interaction and complex psychological motivations.

The Amsirs and the Iron Thorn (1967, aka *The Iron Thorn*) is set on an initially unidentified world colonized by humans, although they live under primitive conditions and must fight for survival against the Amsirs, human-sized and vaguely birdlike aliens who appear to be indigenous to that world. The protagonist is Honor White Jackson, a human warrior. The humans live on the Iron Thorn, a relatively small region which has been engineered to provide breathable air and which is dominated by the Thorn, obviously a spaceship. Outside the Thorn, humans must wear special caps to process the atmosphere, and even then they need to retain a line of sight to the Thorn to keep the cap working properly.

As the story opens, Jackson has just killed his first Amsir after a lengthy hunt. No one had ever told him that the Amsirs could talk and that they used spears. His brother, Black Jackson, meets him secretly when he comes back to the Thorn and White realizes that if he had been wounded, his own brother would have killed him to prevent the rest of the community from knowing that the Amsirs have weapons and are intelligent. Jackson makes no effort to conceal from his brother and the elders that he understands and dislikes their deceit.

Jackson has a long talk with the head Elder, who justifies the lies as necessary to maintaining the stability of their society. He also suggests that Jackson could become his successor and speculates that the Amsirs are also hunting humans and wanted to take him prisoner. Jackson is furious about the falsehoods and deserts his fellows, which leads to his being hunted by them. He kills one of the hunters and then surrenders to an Amsir, who provides him with air, water, and warm clothing. The Amsirs turn out to have their own Thorn, presumably another spaceship, and another construct they call the Object.

The Amsirs want him to find a way to enter the spaceship situated in their territory. Their kind are seriously injured or killed if they try and they do not understand how or why it happens. There is a recorded warning which suggests that this is also a human designed vessel. The Amsirs have no food that he can eat, but they tell him there is edible food in the Object, if he can find a way inside. It is not clear how they know this. The Amsirs also occasionally give birth to mutations that differ from both themselves and humans.

Jackson figures out how to argue with the computer that has locked the Object and gets inside, where the automated systems reactivate and provide medical attention and food, accepting that he is now in command. They also provide a fast track education that includes human history, operation of the spaceship, and knowledge of Earth.

Jackson orders the ship back to Earth – it was on Mars – accompanied by one of the mutants. There he learns that he was part of an experiment in adaptation. The Amsirs are modified humans. The people of Earth have developed a very advanced but decadent civilization, to which Jackson ultimately adapts. The novel has no clear climax and stops rather than ends.

Michaelmas (1977) was the first new novel in a decade and many consider it his best. Laurent Michaelmas is a rather prominent journalist and public figure but his possession of Domino, an advanced artificial intelligence that connects to the worldwide database, makes him effectively the ruler of the world although he is the only one who knows this.

The story opens with the news that Walter Norwood, presumed

dead in a shuttle accident, actually survived and is expected to fully recover. Despite various bits of evidence, Domino and Michaelmas conclude that this is a hoax, that it is impossible that anyone could have survived the explosion of the shuttle. Norwood was slated to lead an expedition to the outer planets and his backup is a Russian. Michaelmas believes that his supposed resurrection is part of an effort by parties unknown to alter the course of human history, although he does not believe that whoever is responsible is yet aware that Michaelmas himself is already manipulating it.

The doctor responsible for the miracle recovery is Professor Limberg and Michaelmas believes he is under the sway of the unknown other influence, but probably not a part of the conspiracy directly. He flies out to Switzerland to cover the story and meets another journalist, an old friend, who bemoans the fact that there are no real causes in the world any longer, that the news stories are less significant to people than they used to be.

There is clandestine work to be done as well. Through Domino, Michaelmas exposes or conceals corruptions and secret deals in order to maintain an international balance of power. Officially, however, he is temporarily assigned to work with Clementine Gervais, another journalist. He suspects that she may have been planted on him by an adversary who has calculated his existence but has not yet identified him. This theory is given support when his old friend is killed in an odd accident and a package from Limberg is secretly routed through another name to avoid the possibility that it might be traced.

Michaelmas recognizes that the major press conference that follows is mostly a farce, that there are tensions hidden from the world between the space authority and Limberg's people. He also discovers that Domino has encountered a peculiar anomaly at the clinic which inhibited his ability to gather and analyze data, and which he has difficulty explaining.

An inside contact tells Michaelmas confidentially that Norwood insists that his shuttle was sabotaged by the Russians so that one of their nationals would take over the command of the planned space project. This is clearly designed to increase tensions between the Soviet Union and the West and is contrary to the efforts of Michaelmas to dampen world unrest and conflict. Domino also reveals that Gervaise nearly died in an accident and spent almost a year at Limberg's clinic.

There is considerable political maneuvering on the international stage. A very clever and subtle bit of sabotage is designed to disable one of the Soviet astronauts but Domino manages to nullify it. Investigators are sure that the crash that killed the journalist was sabotage but they lack proof and decide not to go public, although Domino knows their conclusions.

Limberg and his associates provide what appears to be the Soviet device used to sabotage Norwood's shuttle, but Domino and the space agency have already determined that it is a counterfeit. Michaelmas then confronts Limberg and learns that the professor is in touch with an alien intelligence that believes our world is just an elaborate simulation. It is likely that they exist on Jupiter and that this is why the space program had to be sabotaged. Limberg was using probability manipulation rather than medical treatments to "cure" his patients. Michaelmas has Domino assigned to monitor him for the remainder of his life. He also determines that a rival reporter sabotaged the helicopter that resulted in his friend's death and uses Domino to bankrupt him and ruin his career.

Budrys' final novel was *Hard Landing* (1993). It opens in epistolary fashion with an account of the finding of the body of Neville Spearman, apparently electrocuted by accidentally touching the third rail in a train system near Chicago. Spearman's identity is false, however, and he can only be traced back for less than three years. This is followed by a discussion of the autopsy which found multiple anomalous structures within his body.

Jack Mullica is oddly aware of a man named Selmon who frequently rides the same commuter train as he does, although they do not associate with one another. But there is a news story about a strange object found in a swamp, possibly a space vessel, and Selmon approaches him, worried that this will lead to their identification as aliens. After destroying their instruments, the stranded crew had separated, each making a new life among the people of Earth. The two of them argue and Selmon, who called himself Spearman, fell onto the third rail. That leaves only three of the aliens alive.

Mullica's wife Margery does not know his true origin. Mullica briefly worries that Selmon's death will reveal their existence, but he decides the chances are low and that in any case there is nothing to link the two of them. There is an interlude when we learn that Mullica's race and another, known as methane breathers, are both routinely monitoring activities on Earth because humanity is potentially a significant force once they have expanded into space. They also have a policy of not attempting to rescue anyone who crashes.

Through a series of memoirs and recollections, we learn about the lives of the other castaways, one of whom is believed to have died of injuries sustained in the crash. Another man, Hanig, commits murder and robbery to acquire enough cash to establish himself as a laborer in Denver. The captain, Ravashan, was disloyal to his oath and immediately turned himself in to the American military, to whom he divulged his origin, although it was kept secret from the public. In fact, an ambitious Congressman takes charge for his own personal reasons.

Eventually we learn that Ravashan deliberately caused the malfunction because he knew that he could provide small technological innovations on Earth, earn a fortune, and lead a clandestine but luxurious life. Hanig shows up and accuses Mullica of murdering Selmon. He kills him but Margery returns and pushes Hanig off the balcony to his death. The story ends rather ambiguously with the author speaking directly to the reader and suggesting that he made the whole thing up, which of course he did.

Short Stories

Budrys was a very prolific short story writer during the 1950s. His first short story published was "Walk to the World" (1952). A retired spaceman has never quite lost his desire to see new worlds and he has passed some of that desire on to his son. When human expansion runs into a peaceful but intractable alien civilization, he is asked to come out of retirement to negotiate with them, but the narrator suggests that the outcome might be the beginning of a change in humanity's aggressive instincts rather than a change in the other culture.

One more story appeared that year. "The High Purpose" is a minor piece in which a group of men launch the first spaceship from Earth even though humanity has just been invited to join an interstellar civilization with much more advanced technology that would become available to them. It is a matter of pride rather than necessity.

Several stories appeared in 1953 and Budrys would remain prolific throughout that decade. "The Congruent People" appears at first to be a story of parallel worlds. The protagonist observes some oddities – coats buttoned the wrong way, newspapers that carry variant stories, etc. He impulsively investigates and discovers that this was all designed to lead him to the realization that while most of the world lives in Stage One, a minority has migrated to Stage Two, a civilization within another and completely invisible to the larger population. Several later stories include similar themes.

"Recessional" describes the results of a situation when a small human military outfit is trapped on a planet by a superior enemy force. The narrator attempts to convince the commander in charge of the theater of operations to rescue them, and fails, which provides the author with a chance to expound upon the inevitability of constant crisis and collapse in conventional empire building.

"Protective Mimicry" (aka "The Frightened Tree") starts with the discovery of multiple identical copies of a currency supposedly impossible to counterfeit. The protagonist is sent to the planet where it was found with orders to track down what is probably a matter duplicator. A man named Munger tries to kill him but is thwarted, so the agent and a police officer travel to the native village where he lives. The protagonist is taken captive this time and learns that the natives worship a tree. When the tree is startled by loud noises, it creates scores of duplicates of whatever appears to be the menace. When a fistfight erupts, the agent falls into the tree and there are promptly more than a hundred copies of the agent on hand to capture the criminal. Obviously the story is intended to be humorous, but the logic of the tree is never explained and the ending is telegraphed.

Several of the stories from this period are minor although they occasionally contain interesting ideas. In "Undercrestimation" (a collaboration with Jerome Bixby as Alger Rome) a female fugitive stows away rather improbably on a ship bound for the tiny colony on Mars, which appears to have no room or resources for her. The pilot's infidelity leads to a solution. This is a variation of the classic "The Cold Equations" by Tom Godwin. "Multifarious" describes the visit of an advanced contact team from an aggressive competitive alien race who discover that the now fully cooperative human race will likely absorb his culture because of their more efficient social system. "Little Joe" is the name of an aging merchant starship whose crew come to terms with the fact that it is to be placed in a museum. "The Weeblies" is a rather silly story about a new form of life that threatens to overrun the world until a man discovers a death ray which, unfortunately, kills all the humans as well. A group of astronauts building a space station gets stranded in orbit when a nuclear war breaks out on Earth in "Snail's Pace." "Firegod" is a vignette in which a man plans to shape a civilization so that he can return centuries later, thanks to a time differential, and take over as their god. Instead he is executed as an imposter.

Some of these early stories were more remarkable. "Riya's Foundling" is an oddly touching piece in which a boy with the ability to teleport to other worlds escapes a war ravaged Earth to visit a planet inhabited by mildly intelligent herbivores. Riya is too old to have a mate and is in despair, but she is telepathic and the boy is clearly a child, so she casts him for the part. But he is unsuited for life grazing grass and tries to return to Earth, only to discover that she has mental abilities that prevent him from leaving her until he is an adult. So he teleports the two of them back to the orphanage where he lives.

"The Real People" is a novelette in which a man recovering from an accident has contradictory memories in which his injuries are serious, moderate, or superficial. In a series of scenes that jump around in time and space, the author establishes the fact that most people are pretty much the same and that those few who stand out often feel out of place. Although this seems obvious, the protagonist wonders if his observations of this fact have led him into a bizarre kind of insanity in which he manufactures memories. He consults a psychologist – there is a lengthy and rather interesting discussion of paranoia and delusion – but that only convinces him that he is the only real person and that he is able to change the past if the present does not suit him. To prove it irrefutably, he "invents" a murder that he has committed and then confesses to the police. A good deal of corroborative evidence comes to light. He is convicted and discovers that he cannot change reality this time. The woman he supposedly murdered visits him in jail, tells him that he is only one of several people who manipulate reality, and helps him regain his power. He is nevertheless convinced that he is a god and only when she demonstrates her ability to block his changes does he accept that he is not.

"Blood on My Jets" is a very different type of story. Ash Holcomb is a hired gun working unofficially for the Earth government. In the aftermath of a system wide war, Mars and Venus are dominated by petty warlords and people like Holcomb intervene to keep any one person from acquiring too much power. An old acquaintance – a woman named Pat - offers him a job without providing details and minutes later he is helping her fend off three armed attackers. His instructions are to accept a job ferrying a power plant to Titan. Pat wants to hijack the shipment and give it to one of the warlords. But there is actually no power plant on the ship. The ship itself is experimental and will be fitted on Titan so that it can travel through hyperspace. But Pat is secretly working with the warlord, who has already stolen the technical data from Titan. Holcomb is forced to deal with the warlord, who reveals that he plans to literally destroy the Earth using the new drive. Pat dies helping Holcomb escape. This was not a particularly good story and the climax is very weak.

Fuoss, the protagonist of "Dream of Victory," is an android. He is also dealing with some recurring but nebulous discontent. His last several jobs were eliminated after short intervals. The androids were created when the human race nearly wiped itself out and needed a work force. They are essentially human except that they cannot reproduce. But there has been a change. Androids have become unnecessary. No new ones are being created and those that exist are being shunted out of the work force. There is an effort by some androids to establish themselves as spacemen, but Fuoss undercuts them when he begins to act irrationally and kills the woman with whom he is having an affair.

Budrys proved to be even more prolific in 1954. "To Civilize" is a minor story but it illustrates the growing subtlety of Budrys' storytelling. A group of Earthmen make no protest when they are expelled from an alien world whose people have been judged as capable of shaping their own destiny. "A.I.D." refers to an anti-interrogation device in a very minor story about the use of symbiotes in an interstellar war. "We Are Here" is also quite forgettable. The protagonist manipulates humans with an almost psychic power. One of his subjects is killed and he does not understand why. The story is a satire on consumerism among other things, but it never really takes solid form and wanders considerably, very uncharacteristic for Budrys.

"Scream at Sea" is a much better story, but despite being published in a genre magazine, it is not science fiction. A man and a cat are stuck on a raft after a tanker explodes and sinks. He dies of pneumonia and the cat survives long enough to be rescued by eating his body. "Desire No More" is another minor story about a man whose obsession is to go to the moon. Psychologists decide that he might not be willing to return from space when faced with the awe of the unknown, so they implant memories of a previous moon flight that actually never happened to make him less emotional about it.

"First to Serve" is one of the author's best, told almost entirely from the point of view of a self aware robot. He is a prototype designed by the military and is allowed to overhear arguments about the advantages and disadvantages of proving it various degrees of autonomy. The perfect soldier mode can only be achieved by establishing individuality, and that scares the upper echelon who worry about a robot rebellion. Eventually the project is channeled into an obviously hopeless direction after the robot kills a human being.

"Exotic Dawn" blends SF with fantasy. The protagonist has been marooned alone on a planet for years. Another ship finally arrives with a crew of one, but the marooned man suspects that this is the latest manifestation of the Flying Dutchman, cursed to wander space alone forever. The newcomer convinces him otherwise and cajoles him aboard, which makes him the Flying Dutchman and releases the soul of the man who has been imprisoned aboard for countless generations.

"The End of Summer" considers the consequences of immortality. Christopher Fay has to carry a memory vault which stores the memories he can no longer carry inside his head. Fay has lived for ten thousand years and is a Dilly, short for dilettante. His decision to drive a car without automatics operating is frowned upon by the Homebodies and Workers, and in fact he accidentally kills a young boy's dog while doing so. The world has become a relentlessly safe place, with harnesses in bathtubs and first aid kits everywhere. Fay experiments with his own memories and discovers that human civilization has stagnated and that there is nothing that he can do about it. This is an ambitious story that does not quite achieve its ambitions.

Budrys continued to write short stories prolifically throughout the 1950s, sometimes having two or even three stories in the same issue of a magazine, for which he used a number of pseudonyms including Paul Janvier, Alger Rome, Robert Marner, William Scarff, John Sentry, Albert Stroud, and others. "Nobody Bothers Gus" is a subtle portrait of a superman and one of his best known shorts. Gus Kusevic can perform better than any human athlete and can extrapolate from small amounts of data. He is protected by an aura that makes humans tend to forget about him, which is also his curse because he is unable to hold a job for long. The plot is otherwise almost non-existent. He receives a notice that his property is being seized for a highway extension, and he decides not to make them choose another route, even though he could easily do so, but the story is still quite effective despite a relative lack of progression.

A robot gets stranded on a supposedly uninhabited planet in "In Human Hands" but there is actually a somewhat primitive humanoid race there which is remarkably open to innovation and which is progressing exponentially faster than humans did. The robot becomes an informal guide for them, providing abstract knowledge but allowing them to develop their own technology and customs. A century passes and the race now has technology superior to that of Earthmen, which they discover to their dismay when they return.

"Shadow on the Stars" presents an alien race whose social system is based on paranoia. They are being slowly defeated by a horde of barbarians with spaceships until a mysterious figure arises who leads the fleet to a series of victories. His second in command, who plans to assassinate him, is stunned to discover that he is actually an Earthman in a clever disguise who used his people to defeat the barbarians, and in the process left them much weakened. Budrys would return to this universe, but with different characters.

"Two Sharp Edges" is a somewhat overly sentimental story in which a man discovers that alien humans have been living among us because they virtually destroyed their own world. The vast majority of Budrys' aliens are virtually indistinguishable from humans. "The Strange Room" has some biting commentary on the human tendency to prefer ignorance to knowledge, but is otherwise an implausible story about an alien empire that uses time travel to hide from an emerging humanity.

"Citadel" is another rather strange space opera in which human civilization is spreading through the galaxy, ostensibly with a libertarian form of government although actually the bureaucracy has a very directed policy to manipulate events. The protagonist asserts that humans are successful because of their own major flaw, that their word in an agreement is only valid at that moment because subsequent events change the situation and therefore have different imperatives. The story is surprisingly cynical.

"Just Around the Corner" takes place in an Orwellian future, although the ruling dictatorship is barely holding on to control. When a man with no papers kills a police officer using a bizarre new electrical weapon, both the government and the resistance party are interested. After various efforts by all parties involved fail to succeed, we discover that the man with the weapon is from an alternate world, but the story ends without a clear resolution of any of its conflict. "Thunderbolt" is rather bad. An astronaut takes his experimental ship out of orbit against direct orders, planning to circumnavigate the moon instead, but is snatched by an alien vessel that happens to be traveling through the solar system.

"Thing" is set in the aftermath of a nuclear war. The government has noticed that a formerly sedate citizen has apparently developed superhuman mental powers. During an interview, he explains that he has not, that he picked up an alien parasite that was very unhappy about the war and plans to prevent any new ones. It replicates itself and takes over government officials and presumably world peace is now assured. "Assassin" is a fanciful story in which scientists find a way to allow the "soul" to exist after the death of its body and still interact with the world, and this turns a man into an invincible assassin.

In "Last Stand" a brash young man decides to be the first human to visit another habitable planet and leaves his ship before it officially lands. A storm disrupts his plans to return to the ship – he does not know in which direction to walk – and the very short local day disrupts his sleep patterns. He also has very limited rations and for a long time sees no wildlife. He knows the planet is inhabited but there are no artificial structures and no sign of the indigenes. Eventually a flight of birds provides some fresh meat, but then he has a number of close calls with more dangerous animals over the course of several days. When he reaches a native settlement, he forces one of them to take him by boat to where the spaceship landed, only to discover that it crashed and exploded and that he is alone.

"Terror in the Stars" opens with an alien vessel searching for Earth. The aliens know that humans once existed because a ship full of mummified bodies drifted into their system. They have a hyperspace drive which is occasionally erratic. When they reach Earth they discover that humans migrated to hyperspace and that their ship's passage is causing devastation in the other universe. "Shark" is a very minor story about space pirates and underappreciated veterans. "Watch Your Step" examines the consequences of a devastating interstellar war as observed by an Earthman who is not directly involved.

"The Strangers" is a longish story about a man who discovers that humans are being used as a repository for a race of non-physical beings from another universe who have been caught in what is to them a very slow timestream. He figures out a way to set them free. "In Clouds of Glory" is a sequel to "Shadow on the Stars." Humans are largely content to stay within the solar system, but the Agency continues to physically alter agents to resemble aliens in order to sabotage their operations and increase human influence in other star systems.

"Pagan" is a minor alien invasion story. The alien who lands in a farmer's field uses a ray to transform human prisoners into Earth adapted versions of its own species. The farmer decides that even if these new bodies are improvements, he does not want to be changed. In the fairly amusing "Aspirin Won't Help It" a man develops telekinesis as the result of a viral infection. "The Undiscovered Country" continues the history of humanity which began in "Shadow on the Stars." After centuries of war, only humans and Nilkans still battle to dominate the galaxy. The Nilkans finally "win" by kidnapping humans and incorporating them into their civilization, but in fact the transplanted humans are already planning to revamp the Nilkan culture into a human one, absorbing it from within.

Budrys continued to write frequent stories that included interesting themes that are often treated rather superficially, perhaps with the intention of causing the reader to consider the consequences of the premise. "The Man in the Sky," for example, examines the problems that arise when the first man in orbit dies of natural causes. The space program is eventually restructured to bring his body back to Earth because of popular pressure to honor a hero despite the damage this does to the program as a whole. "The Strength of Ten" consists almost entirely of a conversation between two men who argue about the value of a robot with a mind untroubled by emotions but also uninspired by them. "With a Dime on Top of It" takes the reader along on a suicide mission to drop an atomic bomb on Moscow in a future atomic war. Most of the crew do not know that they cannot fly far enough to escape the blast.

Some stories simply explore a speculative possibility. "The Man Who Always Knew" is able to determine which people are likely to develop new inventions simply by meeting them. "Psioid Charley" is the sequel to "Aspirin Won't Help It." A man who developed telekinesis after catching a bad cold is working at a diner and notices that one of his customers apparently has the same ability. His attempt to confirm his theory results in a panicky scene and the discovery that others in the diner also have telekinesis, that he is apparently a carrier and is spreading it like a virus.

"The Mechanical Man" involves a proposed test of an invulnerable protective suit on the moon. A premature atomic explosion wipes out the test team, except for one technician who happened to be wearing the suit at the time. But the technician is a paranoiac who refuses to get out of the suit. The protagonist must find a way to manipulate the man's mental state. "Middleman" illustrates the fact that the people who know how society functions, the middlemen, are the safest group when governments are violently changed. "Look on My Works" is a somewhat longwinded account of colonists returning to Earth after centuries of isolation and finding that a new and very different society has emerged following an ecological disaster.

"Death Match" has another interesting premise but the story takes too long to develop. On a colony world where people undergo a series of tests to determine their job, a young man discovers that those who pass the most tests and become "nobles" are actually the least happy because of all of the responsibility they must assume. In "Next of Kin" a man invents a machine that will neutralize his brother's psi powers and kill him because his existence constitutes too great a danger to the rest of humanity. But then he realizes that possession of his invention now makes him an even greater danger.

"The Executioner" is one of the best stories from this period. Civilization has collapsed and New York is a separate nation ruled by a theocracy that ruthlessly protects the status of a privileged minority. The protagonist is an aging judge who presides over show trials at which anyone even remotely challenging the status quo is executed. He is, however, a confirmed believer in the religious basis and believes that he is serving god. This leads to a long and well structured conversation between him and his mistress, who points out the fallacies in the system. It is clear that there are at long last signs of a rebellion among the general population and in fact one of the other judges is murdered that same night. He remains a confirmed believer and when he discovers that the system is corrupt, he publicly shoots two other judges to carry out what he believes is justice.

The protagonist of "Silent Brother" is an astronaut who is badly disabled because of a crash. The night after the first starship returns to Earth, he apparently makes extensive modifications to his television set while asleep, though he has no memory of it the following day, and does so after carrying it down into his basement, which would have been virtually impossible given his physical condition. It is obvious that he has become infected with an alien symbiote brought back by the starship, and the degree of his transformation – all of his injuries are soon healed and he can now discorporate his body and slip under doors – is somewhat over the top.

"Lower Than Angels" provides a glimpse of life aboard a commercial exploration starship. The protagonist has recently been hired and is appalled to discover that his crewmates are not heroic figures at all – in fact they are rather disreputable and self-serving. He is sent down to a newly discovered planet to make contact with the natives, who immediately assume that he is a god, no matter how much he tries to convince them otherwise. He is worried that they will be exploited by another human with fewer scruples, so he concocts a plan by which robots are sent to pretend they think the natives are gods, thus teaching them to properly consider offworlders as simply other men.

"The Peasant Girl" is a bittersweet portrait of a man trying to cope with the fact that humans are evolving into something entirely new. "And Then She Found Him" suggests that a new mutation might make some people impossible to notice. A recruiter for a group of these mutants runs into a woman who has that ability, plus the power to force people to do what she wants, so he is forced to kill her because she is undisciplined and dangerous.

"The Burning World" is set in a high tech future world that has become fragmented. The protagonist is a highly placed official in a libertarian state that believes it has established freedom, at least for all of the males. When an upstart politician seems likely to replace his handpicked candidate in an election, he decides to falsify the vote in order to change the results. By his very actions he has proven that there actually is a government, and a corrupt one. An invasion by a neighboring country makes the whole election moot and underscores the inherent weakness of a libertarian society.

"The Shadow Before" shows us a man whose wife begins to falter when her mother moves in and eventually we discover that she is a kind of mental creation that disappears when she is no longer needed. "Lost Love" is a vignette that once again deals with people whom no one can remember moments after meeting them. "The Attic Voice" is a minor piece in which a young man discovers that his recently deceased father was secretly helping a stranded alien, although it has some nicely crafted sentiment.

"The War Is Over" posits a future in which men use an alien symbiote on courier missions. When one of them crashlands on an uninhabited world and the host dies, it moves into a lower animal and infests the entire species, molding them to a single purpose – the construction of a starship to complete the mission – and in doing so provides a kind of rudimentary intelligence that disappears instantly once the ship is launched. "Mark X" also involves symbiotes. The government is trying to develop one that will allow its agents to resist interrogation, but a side effect is that the latest strain turns its hosts completely sane. This is not an advantage for secret agents.

"Cage of a Thousand Wings" is one of Budrys' weakest stories, a kind of parable about witches on other worlds. "Resurrection on Fifth Avenue" revolves around an odd event. A handful of people suddenly find themselves in a deserted future New York City with an apparently human creature who glows and insists he is only five days old. The humans want to go back home but the glowing one wants company and believes he may be a god. "Wonderbird" was written in collaboration with Harlan Ellison. A primitive alien race that was once visited by traveling human entertainers discovers that they are not gods after all when they return and act rudely. "Skimisher" is a vignette about a man from the future who murders people in the present through elaborate accidents.

"Chain Reaction" examines slavery and freedom. The humanoid natives of an unnamed world have long been slaves of the Masters, outworlders who have mental and physical abilities that make them virtually gods. But one day Earthmen, who have equal abilities thanks to technology, capture all of the Masters and initiate the process of freeing the population. Sudden change would be too upsetting, and the humans prefer that the natives feel that they gained their own freedom, so a program of gradual emancipation and uplift is decided upon. Only one of the village leaders knows the truth. But when the freed people begin doing things that are clearly unhealthy, some of the men who were supposed to be simply observing find themselves trying to give orders instead. They eventually find themselves filling the role of the former Masters. This is one of the author's best stories.

"The Ridge Around the World" (aka "Forever Stenn") is a perplexing story about an apparently immortal and invulnerable farmer who survives through the ages until humanity is extinct. It is reminiscent but inferior to "Nobody Bothers Gus." "If These Be Gods" is a longish story about an airliner inadvertently struck by a flying saucer piloted by humanoids from Venus. The story wanders a bit and has no climax but is notable chiefly for the author's adept use of characterization to create a fairly large cast of interesting and well differentiated characters in a very short time.

"The Barbarians" is set in a future where North America has reverted to a medieval lifestyle complete with invading barbarians. One young noble in the league of "civilized" men is nearly killed by one of his allies and wakens to find himself prisoner of the leader of the defeated barbarians. The latter points out that the victors are dividing up the property of their own allies and that if the protagonist were to return home, he would probably be killed out of hand. They end up helping one another, and it is never clear which of the two is actually more civilized.

"The Edge of the Sea" is a very nicely told story of a man

battling a hurricane to salvage what turns out to be an alien probe. He holds onto it when it is carried up to the mother ship. "A World Named Mary" is unmemorable. A man names an uninhabited planet after his rather egotistic wife but the planet literally resents their presence and eventually kills her. "There Ain't No Other Roads" is confusing and trivial. A galactic police officer with amnesia outwits a gang of criminals.

"Infiltration" is a rationalized werewolf story in which aliens trapped on Earth go into suspended animation, but always keep some of their kind awake to watch for any potential rescue. "The Talented Progenitor" is the father of a large number of geniuses in this not quite serious story. The government tracks him down and finds out that it is not his genes that matter. He simply had a talent for finding women who would produce exceptional offspring.

"The Eye and the Lightning" takes place in a future where remote viewing and matter transmission have turned the entire race into paranoid recluses who live in hidden places and wear elaborate disguises when they venture out for supplies. The protagonist survives a remote attack because he has a kind of schizophrenia that made it impossible for his unknown enemy to target his real persona.

"Go and Behold Them" (aka "The End of Winter") starts with the search for a married couple engaged in scientific research in deep space. They are found dead in their ship, which crashed on an artificial world built by a race that was attempting to create life. The dead couple had a secret – she was unwilling to engage in sexual activity – but burying her body on the metal planet appears to have initiated a process that will result in a new form of life.

"Never Meet Again" is a story of alternate worlds. An embittered scientist in a triumphant German Reich moves to an alternate probability – our own history – and finds the wife who died in his original world. His wife betrays him to the Soviet occupiers and he decides that he will have to rebuild his machine and try again. "The Distant Sound of Engines" is a vignette about a man from the future who is seriously injured and attempts to pass on technology to another patient at the hospital, who assumes it is just an illusion.

"Contact Between Equals" is fun but not very logical. An alien has been tricked into providing advanced medical technology by which his captor switches bodies to avoid retribution. But the alien cannot tell humans apart visually and picks the wrong target. "The

Man Who Tasted Ashes" is an assassin who accepts a commission from a secret alien agent to cause an incident which will lead to a nuclear war. He double crosses them and disables one of their ships so that the government can seize it.

"Between the Dark and the Daylight" postulates a crashed colony ship whose occupants have been living inside a large dome for centuries. They have used bioengineering on their children to make them physically capable of living outside the dome, in a world with an alien atmosphere and swarms of actively hostile creatures. The current "captain" has locked off the nursery and the rest of the colonists are restive about his dictatorial manner. When the children are finally released they share the universal hatred for the humans and begin attacking them.

"The Girl in the Bottle" is another vignette. A soldier in a future war believes that his first love is somehow trapped in a glass bottle and is devastated when it is destroyed. "Star Descending" is a slightly opaque story about a service that manipulates space and time to help its clients, until a rival company finds a way to neutralize them. "Man Alone" is actually about two men, crashed on a planet with an abandoned alien city. They are mortal enemies and stalk each other, but one of them has been replaced by a shapechanging alien.

"The Stoker and the Stars" takes place after humans have been defeated in an interstellar war and are largely confined to their own system. An ex-marine has won the respect of his former enemies, however, and is allowed to become a crewman on one of their ships in order to see the galaxy. "Straw" is a rather routine story of political and criminal maneuvering in an undersea city. The sequel is "Due Process." The same protagonist returns, this time to thwart an effort to cripple the main transportation line from the undersea city to the mainland. "The Sound of Breaking Glass" posits a readily available drug that makes people completely suggestible and suggests that this would destroy civilization as everyone would become paranoid.

Most of the monthly science fiction magazines were gone by 1960 and Budrys was increasingly turning his attention to criticism and editing. He published just over a dozen short stories during the next decade, some of which were his best work at that length. "The Rag and Bone Men" serve an alien creature whose matter transmitter malfunctioned, marooning him on Earth and somehow destroying civilization. He manufactures artificial men to serve him while he attempts to rebuild his transportation, but the new device malfunctions as well and it appears humanity is not yet to be free of its presence. "For Every Action" is a vignette about a machine that affects thoughts.

The protagonist of "Die, Shadow!" makes the first flight to Venus but crashes. Fortunately, he has an escape capsule complete with a suspended animation system that will allow him to survive for centuries, hopefully long enough that he will be rescued. When he wakens, millennia have passed and humans have infested the universe while he was preserved in status and viewed as a god. The decision to waken him was a contentious one. He is to participate in a trial by combat to determine the future of a human race that is confused about its purpose and destiny.

"Balloon, Oh Balloon!" is a mildly humorous, almost surreal story perhaps meant as a parody of Ray Bradbury. "Cerberus" is not science fiction despite its appearance in a genre magazine, but is actually a reflection upon the art of storytelling. "Now Hear the Word of the Lord" involves robots from the future trying to prevent the world from being destroyed by a nuclear war. "The Price" is an enigmatic vignette about an immortal discovered while humanity is on the verge of extinction.

"Wall of Crystal, Eye of Night" concerns the rivalry between two businessmen in the future. Sollenar has risked everything on a new venture only to find that his enemy has consulted members of the dying Martian race and perhaps acquired a new device that will bankrupt the protagonist. He decides to kill him and steal the device, but discovers that the Martians also apparently made the other man immortal and virtually invulnerable. An agent is assigned to ensure that Sollenar's investors do not lose their money, an agent who has been deprived of all sensation in order to make him incorruptible. But the Martians sell Sollenar another device which creates a kind of counterfeit reality, and he uses this to restore the agent's senses and turn him against his employers.

In "All for Love" (aka "For Love") humanity is losing a war against alien invaders who have arrived in a single, gigantic spaceship and whom no human has ever seen since their weaponry and scouting vehicles appear to be remote controlled. The protagonist is assigned to drive a virtually invisible weapons carrier up to one of its legs and set a bomb that will topple the ship. The bomb does not do as much damage as planned, but it provides proof that another such attack will likely succeed since the ship is now off balance. The reader never finds out whether they are right, however, or what is inside the ship because the story ends there.

"The Last Brunette" has no fantastic element. A man's car breaks down in a small town and he has an intense encounter with a local woman. "The Master of the Hounds" is not SF either and was filmed as *To Kill a Clown*. A married couple discovers that their new neighbor is a famous ex-soldier who was notorious for his actions at a prisoner of war camp. He has two dogs who have been trained to kill and he uses them to make the couple his virtual slaves.

Budrys wrote even fewer stories during the 1970s. Two of them are vaguely related to the novel, *Michaelmas*. "A Scraping at the Bones" starts when a dead body is found in the sewer system of a gigantic apartment complex. There are odd things about the victim, who was a resident, but who did not always register on its security surveillance. The police officer investigating realizes that he was murdered by someone who coveted some of the dead man's living space. The only connection to *Michaelmas* is that the policeman watches his news program. "The Nuptial Flight of Warbirds" is set in the same world but Michaelmas makes no appearance. It is mostly an air combat adventure story with the revelation that it is all an entertainment and not genuine. The story barely qualifies as science fiction.

"Players at Null-G" was a collaboration with Theodore Cogswell and Ted Thomas. Three men develop an anti-gravity device but something goes wrong and it destroys several buildings. Fortunately the owner is convinced that it was a sudden tornado and he is happy to collect the insurance. They realize later that they have sent a pulse of antigravity out into the universe and that it might create havoc somewhere else.

"The Silent Eyes of Time" deals with a kind of time travel. Clint Gallard retired from the corporation he formerly headed, but is asked to return to deal with the discovery of a machine that allows objects to be brought back from the future. The bulk of the story consists of efforts to prevent the news from getting to the public or the government despite the fact that several employees know part or all of what has happened. Then the limitations are explained – he can only travel four years forward and so far has not encountered his future self. He purchases the items he brings back. Gallard waits until he has moved forward again, then turns off his equipment so that he cannot return to the present, which solves the problem for at least a few years.

The 1980s saw even fewer stories. "The Name of the Game" is a lvignette. Two men approach a bizarre artifact in the wilderness and both are taken inside by some odd mechanism, one of them dying in the process, and the other finds himself trapped. "That Fearful Symmetry" is even shorter and describes the creation of an artificial being who is miffed that he does not look like a literal angel. "What Befell Mairiam" is an odd fantasy in which a warlock tracks down the woman who stole his finger, and its magical ring, which prevents him from holding back a barbarian horde.

There was a flurry of stories during the 1990s, but most of these appeared in *Tomorrow* magazine – which Budrys edited and published - under pseudonyms, and it is not clear if these were new or old stories he had not previously sold. Two other stories appeared in original anthologies. "Living Alone in the Jungle" is a vignette about an invulnerable man who is targeted by a killer. "Grabow and Collicker and I" is a very short piece about soldiers who are patched up and sent back into battle even after suffering fatal wounds.

In "Starlight" the captains of three ships full of embryos intended to colonize new worlds discover that they have entered an alternate universe. One of them decides to colonize Earth, which never developed apes, but the other decides this would be wrong because a different form of life, though not yet intelligent, has become dominant there and she destroys all of the ships. "Explosions!" is an enigmatic short tale in which it appears that Vikings are plotting to create a mythical external enemy to unite themselves but it is actually the future and not the past. "Jeever's Lost World" is about a man living alone in an abandoned city who is annoyed when the near passage of other humans activates the city's defenses which are disruptive to the peace and quiet he values.

"Time and Space" is another vignette, this one about two lonely people who are kept apart because of the antipathy of matter and antimatter. "At Times, an Island" describes a time shift that causes an island to appear where there should be open water. The inhabitants of the island have a superior technology. "The Woman Who Blew Up the World" did so because she felt that the entire population of a colony world supported a system that abused women. "Kinkajou Nine" presents an alien race which has settled many planets, none of which have space travel, and humans discover that it is an experiment set up to observe visitors. None of the stories from the 1990s was particularly memorable and most of them are vignette length.

Closing Note

The Regency edition of *Some Will Not Die* announced plans to publish a mainstream novel by Budrys involving prison life to be titled *Each Man Kills*. The publisher went out of business before the title appeared in print, but Budrys later asserted that the novel had eventually been published. There is a 1962 novel of that title, which would be in the right time frame, as by Sanford Bayer, but it does not involve a prison and is stylistically dissimilar to Budrys' work. If it did in fact appear as a book, it was probably under another title and byline that has not yet been identified. Judith Merril also mentioned in 1967 that Budrys was working on a suspense novel, but that also never appeared.

INDEX OF TITLES

178

9 781796 970302